Treasury of
German Dolls
Album 1

Lydia Richter

Treasury of
German Dolls
Album 1

HPBooks®

China, height 19-3/4 inches (50cm).
Boy doll made between 1850 and 1860.

Notice: The information in this book is true and complete to the best of our knowledge. All recommendations are made without guarantees on the part of the author or HPBooks®. The author and publisher disclaim all liability in connection with the use of this information.

Publisher: Rick Bailey
Editorial Director: Randy Summerlin
Editor: Judith Schuler
Art Director: Don Burton
Book Assembly: Barry Myers
Book Typography: Cindy Coatsworth, Michelle Claridge
Translation: Ruth A. Lewis and John S. Lewis
Technical Consultant: Mildred Seeley

HPBooks®
P.O. Box 5367
Tucson, Arizona 85703
(602) 888-2150
ISBN: 0-89586-328-6
Library of Congress Catalog Card Number: 84-80438
©1984 Fisher Publishing Inc.
Printed in U.S.A.

Originally published in Germany as *Deutsche Porzellanpuppen: Puppen Album 1.*
©1980, 1983 by Verlag Laterna magica GmbH and Co.

ACKNOWLEDGMENTS
For the loan of some of the dolls and accessories, the author would like to thank: Mrs. Roswitha Schaad, Mrs. Gabriele von Eicken, Mrs. Ulrike Zweig-Graefenhahn, Mrs. Ursula Jorde, all of Munich; Miss Agnes Boegner, of Neustadt a. Rbg. and Miss Christiane Hermelink, of Stuttgart.
Doll clothes from old material were made by Mrs. Gertrud Stangl of Munich and Mrs. Margarete Schmidt, of Diessen/Ammersee.
Technical Advice: Mrs. Roswitha Schaad.
Editorial Collaboration:The contributions on pages 10 to 14 and 28 to 31 were written by Mrs. Dorothea Roth.
Photographs: All photographs are by Joachim F. Richter, except those on pages 4, 47, 49, 51, 54, 58, 59, 70, 78, 86, 96, 97 by Hans Graf; pages 29, 35, 106, 107, 110 by Mrs. Roswitha Schaad; pages 8, 9, 15, 22, 23 by Mrs. Christiane Hermelink; pages 77, 82, 116 by Lydia Richter.

From a book of
poems, 1889

TABLE OF CONTENTS

Bisque, Armand Marseille, both marked
No. 370.
These dolls were made around 1900.

Joy of Collecting

I want to tell you of my personal impressions, experiences and motivation to collect dolls because I enjoy this hobby. In using the word *hobby*, I am jumping to the middle of my story. I regard myself as a keeper and preserver of beautiful porcelain pieces, and I do not collect them only to possess beautiful things.

I identify myself with those who do not collect as an end in itself, but collect as an enjoyable hobby. For many people, doll collecting is a hobby, and this is understandable. Dolls were playmates, and it did not matter if dolls were made of fabric or porcelain—we loved them. Dolls consoled us in our times of sorrow, were our friends when we needed them and even helped us fall asleep.

My dolls, along with parents, siblings and friends, were part of my life until I was 13. Then they were taken away by my well-meaning parents who told me, "You are too big to play with dolls. We are giving them to our little nieces."

What brought joy to my cousins brought sorrow to me. I was not only sad, but I had lost a piece of my childhood. I was robbed of my hobbies. For a long time, my dolls had been more than toys. I had crocheted caps for them, knitted their jackets and dressed them with old necklaces to make them beautiful.

Why have I told you this story? Because love for the toys of our childhood is so deeply rooted in us we still love them and find them beautiful. Our perspective has hardly changed, because we still want our dolls to be beautifully dressed and have lovely accessories. Toys that once brought us joy can become a hobby for us.

I had forgotten the dolls in my life until I had a daughter of my own. When she was born, we bought her simple, unbreakable dolls. Later, we purchased two Käthe Kruse dolls. I did not think about starting a collection, but dolls had returned to my consciousness.

I became interested in collecting when I found some beautiful bisque dolls at flea markets and in antique stores. Reservations about not being taken seriously as a collector or being regarded with scorn were destroyed by the fascination of radiant glass eyes and beautiful bisque heads.

At a flea market, I bought my first collector's item. I chose a bisque doll that fit my budget, with a head that looked good to me. Her costume was filthy. Much of the paint had flaked off her body, and her hair was completely matted.

My first impulse was to trade her old wig for a beautiful new one. The clerk said she would give it to me at no additional cost, but I decided against it. I am glad I kept her old mohair wig, because every collector wants to recapture the original condition of her dolls.

When I got her home, I washed her. I carefully combed and brushed the wig with a soft brush and was delighted with the results. After I finished combing the old wig, it was more beautiful than the new one.

Next, the doll had to be dressed. I had a dress made from white fabric and underwear made from easy-care fabric. In this condition, I showed it to a collector friend, who had not liked the doll originally. From my friend, I learned I had to find old patterns and fabrics for the costume to preserve the charm and personality of my old doll. Reproduction costumes, which are *exact* copies of old costumes, are beautiful on old dolls.

In this first phase of my collecting, someone told me it made no sense to buy dolls. This person felt it was senseless because dolls are expensive

Bisque, Simon & Halbig, marked *SH 1079/12 DEP*.
Doll dressed in orange-brown clothes was made in 1892. She has a bisque swivel head and is posed as a magician with character doll by Otto Reinecke.

Bisque, Kämmer & Reinhardt, Simon & Halbig, marked 122.
German baby doll in cradle is attended by her French doll aunt, Unis France. Wrought-iron cradle was made around 1910.

and would eventually be played with by children. This person did not understand that collectors regard themselves as protectors. We must protect these works of art against destruction to give joy to others.

Many dolls are in showcases or on shelves in people's homes. If you want to present yours in the style of a particular time, collecting can be expanded to include carriages, stools, cradles, beds and horses. Old necklaces can be draped on some dolls and old brooches can be pinned on others. Many things can be handmade, such as earrings from wire and old glass beads. See HPBooks' *Doll Costuming* by Mildred and Colleen Seeley for more information on costumes and accessories.

Buying accessories for my collection completed my joy in collecting. But I had to learn restraint. One day I saw a beautiful silk doll umbrella with a carved handle. Other people had tried to buy it. The salesgirl said if she were to sell the umbrella to me, she would anger those whose offers she had refused. I was disappointed, but later I had a chance to buy a colorful cotton umbrella that complemented one of my dolls.

Some people collect things because they are a good investment. For others, it is necessary to make a sacrifice to have a collection or hobby. A dedicated collector is ready to go on a trip to buy an article of clothing or piece of jewelry or to fulfill other wishes.

Today, dolls are often regarded as antiques, and their value has increased greatly. This is good for those who own valuable collections. Those who are just beginning often regard the prices of today's collectables as excessive.

In these activities, we establish closer bonds with our childhood, and we are fortunate for that. The motivation to collect dolls is more diverse than it may seem. For me, an important aspect is the contact with other collectors and people interested in dolls. Private shows, doll clubs and people who are knowledgeable about dolls offer interesting exchanges of ideas and new friendships. For more information about beginning a doll collection, see HPBooks' *Doll Collecting for Fun & Profit,* by Mildred and Colleen Seeley.

I allowed some of my dolls to be photographed. I found the pictures so beautiful I was inspired to write this book. It was necessary to change some clothes, to decorate other costumes and to arrange dolls in beautiful scenes. This gave me pleasure and joy. Collecting dolls has given me another unusual result—it has allowed me to introduce my collection to you.

Lydia Richter

The Goal of this Doll Album

As you begin collecting dolls, you may find many false bargains. Ignorance and inexperience are the prime causes of problems for beginning collectors. Knowing some facts will help you be more informed and thus avoid making mistakes.

Porcelain-Head Dolls

This book deals primarily with porcelain-head dolls, including parian, china and bisque. These dolls, especially those with bisque heads, are among the most popular, frequently collected dolls. To provide you with a cross section, I wrote one book on porcelain dolls of German origin. I wrote two other books dealing with other dolls that are popular with collectors. See HPBooks' *Treasury of French Dolls* and *Treasury of Kathe Kruse Dolls*. It was simple to choose these books. Germany and France dominated the world market for porcelain dolls. Writing these books was sensible because some people collect only German dolls, others collect only French ones and still others are interested in Käthe Kruse dolls.

Handbook

This book provides you with information needed to start your collection. It warns you, as a beginning collector, of problems you may encounter. This book answers questions and shows doll markings.

If you are unknowledgeable about collecting, you must inform yourself in a fast, systematic way of the differences between china, parian and bisque. You must understand different conditions of hair, eyes, mouth and body. Confusing terms, such as *open-closed mouth, marked, all-bisque* and others are explained. Distinctions between shoulder-head, turned-head and swivel-head dolls, character dolls, exotic dolls and others are explained. Pictures help clarify details for you.

Picture Book

Use this book as a picture book with captions and text. Pictures of dolls on right-hand pages are full-face or bust portraits. Detail is presented in a caption. If pictures give joy to you, their presentation is worthwhile.

Dolls with bisque heads were toys, and today they are coveted collectables and considered antique. As you go through this book, you will notice two pages devoted to each doll. This is to present necessary information with a moderate number of pictures.

Dolls are presented on the left-hand page to show and describe clothing, hats and accessories. To vary presentations that are repeated, dolls are shown wearing different wigs or different clothes. This is in keeping with the custom of their time and with the conventions of the industry. Doll makers produced the same body with different heads, wigs and clothing.

Parian, 19-3/4 inches (50cm).
Unmarked turned-head parian doll made between 1860 and 1870. Forearms and lower legs are bisque, and body is cloth. Hair is molded.

From Simple to Exclusive

This book gives you a wide spectrum of dolls. Simple, inexpensive ones were beautiful and loved, and they are presented in many varieties. Extravagant, rare, expensive dolls, such as No.117A by Kämmer & Reinhardt and Simon & Halbig, shown on page 107, or No.1448 by Simon & Halbig, shown on page 111, are included. To make a cross section possible, my collection was supplemented with dolls owned by other people.

Variety of Dolls

This book is oriented to the interests of collectors. Different sections provide a valuable guide for users and collectors. You will find pictures of many types of dolls, such as baby dolls, character dolls, exotic dolls, Victorian dolls or knickknack dolls. Each picture is accompanied by a description.

Knickknacks

Collecting knickknack dolls in many colors has become popular. Many collectors like tea dolls, half-dolls, all-bisque dolls and other unique dolls. Appearances range from lovely and gracious to charming and sexy, and they testify to the diversity of fashion. There is a special area of collecting that deals with these dolls, and we present a general overview on pages 146 and 147.

Cultural History

This book describes china, parian and bisque dolls, wigs and clothes. It shows dolls in beautiful pictures. By reproducing old prints, photographs, post cards, newspaper and book illustrations, poems and stories connected with dolls, we document cultural history. This helps round out the theme of the book. Perhaps these other items will appeal to people who have not been infected with collecting fever.

Photography

Photographs in this book were done by amateurs. Pictures similar to the ones shown here can be done by someone who has technical knowledge of photography. A medium-format camera is suitable for producing studio pictures. We used a Mamiya 645/1000 S with a standard 100mm ƒ-2.8 with a tripod and flash capability. We used a Multiblitz Ministudio 202 with a flash meter. If you want to produce a soft-focus effect, use a Rodenstock Imagon soft-focus lens or similar attachment. In addition to the enjoyment of collecting dolls, you may enjoy photographing them.

Bisque, probably Kling, 21-3/4 inches (55cm).
Bisque turned-head doll from around 1880. Doll has leather hands, and body is cloth. Hair is molded.

Dolls as an Image of Man

Among ancient peoples, and in the religions and games of most primitive cultures, dolls were regarded as the image of man. Egyptians played with movable wood ones as early as 2000 B.C. They dressed dolls in clothes and made dollhouses for them. Tiny marble figures were found in graves of ancient Greek children. Archaeologists believe tiny marble figures were toys.

Clay figures were popular in ancient Greece. Greek maidens consecrated them for the marriage of Artemis, and Roman maidens offered them to Venus.

Among primitive peoples, doll idols were carved from roots, bones, amber, lead and shaped in clay. Clay was a particularly good medium for shaping a human image.

Dolls have been known and loved as toys. Those that are popular collectors' items today first appeared in the second half of the 19th century and the first decade of the 20th century.

Ancient Dolls

It is fascinating to follow the development of dolls. As a prehistoric figure, a doll was often naked and primitively formed. Features were marked on the face, and hair was sketchily indicated. Usually only the upper body was shaped, while the lower part of the body resembled a formless lump. Some dolls were made of stamped metal and are the ancestors of tin soldiers. Dolls began to be made of better materials. Marble was joined by alabaster, and limestone was surpassed by schist.

Dolls were often made in feminine forms. Researchers relate this to the predominance of matriarchies in early cultures. Dolls of primitive peoples were not made for children. Half-fetish, half-idol, they were used as household gods for the worship of ancestors. Dolls were magical and had a mystical aura. For early man, they represented the life of the divinity. The Christian church took control of ancient legends as pictures of gods became statues of saints.

Collection of Hopi Kachina dolls

Girl with doll and doll cradle. Woodcut was made around 1540.

Dolls from the French Empire, 1800 to 1810

Copperplate engraving of children of Herzog family of Orleans. Engraving by Joullain, copied from painting by Coypel, around 1760.

Child with nun doll. Engraving by J.B.S. Chardin.

Ancient dolls, which appeared lifelike and realistic with movable limbs and human-hair wigs, have been found in ancient Egyptian graves. Greeks were familiar with clay dolls, which they painted and decorated with accessories. Doll coiffures were beautifully styled. The double role of dolls must not be overlooked—they were toys and religious idols. Dolls were given to Hera, Artemis or Aphrodite at the time of a girl's entry into adolescence. Giving up the dolls symbolized the end of the girl's childhood.

Greece had a flourishing toy industry in Sardis, the capitol of Lydia. In addition to dolls with clay limbs, wood, ivory and wax dolls were made.

The Romans used dolls as offerings for weddings and burials. Dolls of wood, clay and ivory found their way to the temple before their owner's wedding or burial.

In ancient Rome, many doll mothers dressed their doll children. From the fine, artistic shaping of the doll's bodies, we have been able to deduce a little about their outfits, which have not survived. Background color of gypsum dolls was white. Coloring was finished with careful, realistic painting of the face. Hair was black, shaped and piled high, as was the style for women of ancient Rome. Belongings included furniture, jewelry and utensils—a miniature household.

Early dolls were found in other advanced cultures in South America. Before Spanish colonists arrived, female dolls of pure gold were found in children's graves in Peru. Figures of boys were made of silver and may have been dressed in clothes. Dolls of Incan maidens, wood-and-straw dolls and baby dolls with clay heads and cloth wrappings were found, along with cradle boards.

Many folk-art museums have dolls from primitive peoples. In Australia, Aborigines acquired from civilization a knowledge of dolls as the image of man. Dolls from India were often used as fetishes in rituals. Feathers were used on leather-clothed wood images of men and animals to bring their owners luck. Africans made jeweled ritual dolls, which were seldom played with by children. Medicine men, whose magical powers could be transferred to dolls, used them as fertility symbols.

It was a long road from religious cult figures to dolls in the nursery. Young children have always had the desire to surround themselves with doll playmates. Dolls gave expression to a child's fantasy world. They lived and played with a child in his or her miniature social life.

The transition from fetish to toy was easy. Ashanti maidens still carry flat-cut wood dolls on their backs rather than in their arms as a sign they soon hope to bear their own children. Girls are prepared by their dolls for their role as mother.

People of the far north, especially Eskimos, use dolls in their boats as good-luck charms. They do not decorate them with expensive furs and skins but use pieces of flotsam, jetsam and walrus teeth.

Dolls in the Middle Ages

For information about the Middle Ages in Europe, which was a time of flourishing doll culture, we must depend on various sources. Our knowledge of dolls of princes and princesses is verbal and has been passed down by tradition.

Information about dolls has been preserved through stories and by publication of woodcuts. One book shows illustrations of a doll maker working in his shop. The book is called *Hortus Sanitatis* and was published at the end of the 15th century in Mainz, Germany. The book provides evidence of a trade in jointed wood dolls. We see them taking shape under the cutting knife of a craftsman.

Doll maker from Weigel, 1698

In Nuremberg, many clay dolls were found under some pavement in the middle of the 19th century and were as large as 19-3/4 inches (50cm) in height. Their clothing and hairstyles are similar to images of adults from the middle of the 15th century.

Dolls of the Middle Ages were not all female or all from the female point of view. They were made as images of childhood and sweetness. Dolls came to be regarded as infants in swaddling clothes.

Some dolls were made in other images. They were created in the image of nuns, monks and priests and were popular, especially in Italy. With their religious dolls, children reenacted the Mass or performed other rituals. Tiny religious accessories, such as candlesticks and incense burners, were often made of tin.

These discoveries confirm Nuremberg's early reputation as an important toy center. The guild roster of 1413 lists a *Dockenmacher*—doll maker—a name used by Wolfram von Eschenbach. The expression remained in use for another 300 years, until the Latin-derived name *puppe*, meaning doll, came into general use.

Martin Luther spoke of his wife as a "hubsoher Tocke," meaning a charming doll, and in a *Woman's Lexicon* of 1715, the words *docke* and *puppe* were used.

Even with the increasing number, dolls for children were not popular. Dolls looked like miniature adults, with stiff smiles and narrow-cut clothing. They were the image of adults, not the children for whom they were intended.

Models of Fashion

The model for a doll was not a child but an adult woman. Dolls were models for fashion, and popular clothing styles were displayed on them. In Paris, which was a fashion center, it was customary for the queen to send to other courts beautifully dressed dolls as ambassadors of fashion. In this way, a picture of Paris haute couture was shown to others.

Doll maker from Weigel, 1698

A court embroiderer of Charles V was paid 459 francs for a doll wardrobe he designed. Isabeau de Baviere, who came from Bavaria as queen to the French court, sent her daughter, the English Queen Isabelle, a doll to show latest French fashions. It was life-size so the daughter could try the clothing on herself. Kings used fashion dolls to gain popularity with their mistresses.

In the 18th century, exportation of fashion dolls became a lucrative business for doll makers and Parisian fashion houses. Dolls were sent as mannequins of fashion to England, Germany, Italy and Spain. Even America awaited the arrival of the newest fashion dolls from Europe.

Around the middle of the 19th century, fashion magazines appeared that carried pictures of the newest fashions. Women of high society no longer wanted porcelain and bisque dolls with wardrobes as expensive as their own.

Wood Dolls

Until porcelain dolls were produced, wood ones were made in areas with large forests because material was readily available. Dolls called *limb men* were made and could be posed in any position. They were used by painters to help make groups of figures for paintings. Many wood dolls came from the woodworking cities of Salzburg and Regensburg.

In the 17th century, painted wood dolls with attached, carved arms and sharp noses appeared in Thuringia. Their slender waists distinguished them from those from the Tyrol. Fashion dolls came from upper Bavaria. From the heavily forested Grödner Valley, peddlers brought carved dolls to Bavaria and Italy. Often wood faces were layered with bread dough, then baked, which made them chubby and lifelike.

The Dutch began making wood dolls similar to Tyrolean ones that were exported to England. In England, a doll was made called the *Queen Anne doll.* It was popular during the reign of the English Queen Anne and into the 19th century. The doll had a high forehead and strong cheeks. It was used as a standard of beauty for many years.

While still a princess, Queen Victoria was an admirer of wood dolls. Although wax and parian were popular, she loved the Dutch wood dolls. Her collection of 132 different 3- to 12-inch dolls (8 to 30cm) was personally cataloged, and today it is still on display in Kensington Palace. She costumed many of them herself.

Wax Dolls

Wax dolls were more intricate and lifelike. Because they were molded, modeled or cast, they were easy to color. Often only the head and hands were made of wax. Catholic countries, with votive offerings made of wax, led in the manufacture of wax dolls. Even as early as the 17th century, Daniel Neuberger of Augsburg produced beautiful wax dolls.

In England, which had developed a tradition of wax dolls, an Italian family named Montanari became known for their charming wax dolls. These dolls were among the most beautiful dolls of this type and were valued for their quality. Limbs and head were molded individually, then cast as a single piece. Eyelashes and eyebrows were set with great care, and hair was implanted in the head with a hot needle.

Another Italian family moved to England and became famous for its wax dolls. The Pierotti family made dolls with dark, softly glowing complexions and tufted, implanted hair.

From the Fashion Gallery, 1780

Copperplate engraving of *My doll,* by Noel of Paris, 1806

Copperplate engraving of *My sister looks at my beautiful doll,* by Noel of Paris, 1806

Papier-Mâché-and-Wax Dolls

Papier-mâché-and-wax dolls found their way from England to Europe. They had delicate faces with a fine wax coating, human hair eyebrows and eyelashes, and parted blond hair. Bodies were made of white linen, then stuffed.

In contrast, German wax dolls were inexpensive. A finished, painted papier-mâché head was coated with a thin layer of wax. Duchess Luise Leonore of Saxony created a new export for the Sonneberg wood-doll industry because of her patent for the use of this material in 1805.

In 1820, Sonneberg model maker Martin Heidler obtained a patent for easy-to-shape papier-mâché material. It became possible to shape it the same way as porcelain in gypsum molds. The famous Sonneberg waxed papier-mâché *Täufling*, a baptismal infant doll, was popular for many years in England around the middle of the 19th century.

Heinrich Stier created a papier-mâché head with a flesh-colored wax coating. It was dusted with white powder to give it a soft babylike color. Twenty years later, Stier developed a material that was washable and heat-resistant.

Hairstyles

The progress of porcelain dolls, which appeared around 1800, did not slow. Dolls had painted womanly facial expressions and molded, tightly twisted curls. In 1830, there were many different hairstyles. Constantly changing hair fashions are used as a guide for dating dolls by collectors. For example, in 1860, chignons were a popular style. In 1890, bangs were in vogue.

Dolls from the time of the French Revolution shown in a toy catalog. From *History of Toys*, by Henry René d'Allemagne.

English paper doll, made around 1800

China, Parian and Bisque

When we speak of *porcelain* dolls, it is important to distinguish among china, parian and bisque.

China is highly glazed, hard porcelain. Parian is unglazed porcelain fired without an application of paint. Parian looked smooth and lifelike. China and parian dolls were made as shoulder-heads and turned-heads. A movable neck joint was first used in the middle of the 19th century.

A third type of porcelain is bisque. It is fired or baked until it changes chemically. It does not have a glaze or shine. Bisque was produced in quantity in France. Luxurious dolls, called *poupées de luxe*, were made of bisque and quickly became popular; they are still popular today. The development of bisque dolls has been attributed to France. German doll makers created beautiful works of art at the same time.

China Head

China, which was discovered centuries ago, was rediscovered around 1840 by German and Danish doll makers. At the Industrial Exposition of 1845 in Vienna, the firm of Lippert & Haas introduced doll heads made by the Schlaggenwald Porcelain Factory. According to one report, the curator of the Sonneberg Toy Museum once displayed a doll head of china that has been dated between 1780 and 1790.

China is not beautiful. Its shine gives dolls a cold beauty that has little appeal to children. Heads were not carefully finished or painted so dolls are not as beautiful as bisque. China dolls with cloth bodies were called *Nanking Dolls*.

Parian

In 1842, the Copeland firm of England created parian porcelain, called *parian* for short. It was called parian because it glowed the same as Parian marble cut on the island of Paros. The visible feature that distinguishes parian from china is parian's mat surface.

You can often determine if a doll is made of parian by looking at it closely. If bare places, such as those not covered by paint, are white, the material is parian.

Parian dolls usually had painted blond hair. Those with black hair were not made often. Parian dolls had molded hair with beautiful molded bows, flowers or hats, such as the Victorian bonnet on the doll on page 45.

Although it was customary to paint eyes, a few parian heads had glass eyes set in them. Ears were often pierced.

Bisque

Between 1860 and 1870, the first bisque dolls were made in France. They had mat skin and peach-colored faces. Parian dolls became less popular when bisque was made in large production runs by French and German firms in the early 1870s.

Bisque was fired twice, but not glazed. The first firing produced a hard, white porcelain that was painted, then fired a second time. This resulted in a bond between color and porcelain. The other distinction between parian and bisque is the color of the porcelain. Parian is white and bisque is tinted pink, which more closely resembles the color of human skin.

China, 11 inches (28cm).
Early doll, probably of German origin, with china shoulder-head, wood torso, upper arms and legs, and china forearms and lower legs. Doll can be moved because of hinges in upper arms and legs. Right hand is closed, and left hand is open. Made between 1840 and 1850.

Anatomy of a Doll

Head

Many children's tears have been shed over a broken doll, and collectors have cried over a similar mishap. Porcelain breaks easily and must be handled with caution. Hairline cracks and fissures diminish a doll's value significantly. This is especially true for cracks on the face.

Because of these problems, lift the wig and look through the head with a flashlight. In most bisque dolls, the head is open on top for setting eyes and teeth. This opening is closed with cardboard or cork, called a *pate*, that covers the wig completely. Various holes at the edge of the head reduce the weight of the doll for export or are used to attach the body and wig.

Dolls with closed heads were called *bald-head.* French Belton-type dolls had eyes set in place from below. When looking at a head, see how it was bound to the body.

A shoulder-head doll has head, neck, breast and shoulders in one piece. Because of this construction, the head does not move.

A swivel-head doll has a one-piece head and neck. The head-and-neck piece turns in the socket of the shoulderplate or in a body.

A third variation is the turned-head doll. The head, neck and shoulders are one piece. The head is molded so it slightly tilts or turns to one side, but the head does not move.

A fourth variety is the flange neck, which has a broad place at the base of the neck with holes for fastening it to a cloth body with cord. The head is bound to the body and does not move. This type of neck was often used on baby dolls.

Shoulder-head doll has head, neck and shoulders made in one piece, and head cannot be moved.

Eyes

Eyes give a doll individuality. Many types of eyes were used, such as flat, painted eyes and eyes painted on hollows with concave iris and pupil, called *intaglio* eyes. Fixed and moving sleep eyes moved through the use of a lever and counterweight. Roguish eyes, see the Googly on page 117, were popular. Flirty eyes looked normal and could cast a sidelong glance, such as those on the No. 117N doll on page 109. Paperweight eyes, especially those made by Jumeau, were often used.

Paperweight eyes were invented by the English and first made in Bristol in 1849. Eyes appeared to have depth and color similar to paperweights.

Eyelashes were often painted, but other materials were used for the upper lid, such as hair, see page 91; fur, see page 79; and thread, see page 81.

Mouth

A doll's mouth is important. It gives her a characteristic appearance and determines whether she smiles mysteriously or with melancholy, whether she looks at the world in a lovely way or stupidly.

Early bisque dolls usually had a closed mouth. Today these dolls are rare and valuable. People later found an open mouth with teeth more attractive. Relatively rare, and not pretty, were baby dolls with open, crying mouths.

An open-closed mouth was introduced. The mouth, tongue and teeth were molded to make the mouth appear open. In reality, there is no opening to the interior of the mouth. We call mouths *open-closed* when the space between the upper and lower lips is only partially painted.

Pouty mouths were used on German bisque-character dolls, which are famous for their variations in mouth shaping and painting. For example, the round whistling mouth allowed a child to feed her doll a bottle.

In 1910, many character dolls, such as No.117N of Kämmer & Reinhardt and Simon & Halbig, page 109, or No.1448 of Simon & Halbig, page 111, were made more beautiful because of the dark-red midline between lips.

Experienced collectors can often identify a doll maker from the painting of mouths, which is useful for distinguishing between German and French dolls. With French bisque dolls, the artist was a subtle painter. The contours of a mouth were drawn with a feather brush in various ways. Sometimes they used continuous lines or two tiny bows on the upper lip and two on the lower lip. In rare cases, small dots were used.

Colors of mouths ranged from delicate pink to dark red. Usually the mouth was painted with two colors. After 1900, painting mouths became simpler. The mouth was painted uniformly with red color, often without any toning or contours. Bisque dolls with firmly closed mouths, such as No.1833 by Simon & Halbig, are rare.

Ears

In most cases, ears were cast in a mold with the head. Some heads are found with molded, pronounced ears. Dolls with pierced ears are popular because they can wear beautiful earrings.

Hair

Wigs were rare on china and parian dolls. Instead of wigs, hair was painted on or molded, then painted.

For bisque dolls, wigs were made of lamb's wool, human hair or goat hair, called a *mohair wig*. Lambskin wigs were made from fleece of baby lambs.

Human-hair wigs cost the most because they were hand tied. This was done by tying three or four long hairs together, then threading them through a gauzelike fabric. Strands were tied in a knot, which gave a tuft of six or eight hairs. Hand-tied human-hair wigs are rare today.

To make mohair wigs, goat hair was boiled, dyed and made into threads. Threads were worked into tresses, and tresses were made into a wig by sewing them on a fabric cap. If a curly style was desired, hair was curled on a small wood stick.

Before placing a finished wig on the doll, the open head was closed with a head covering, called a pate. A pate was made of cardboard in Germany and cork in France.

Today when wigs are attached, hard-setting glue is used so it is difficult to remove wigs. Wig removal can often damage a head. A soluble glue or weak glue, such as rubber cement, is better to use.

Manufacture of wigs was taken over by machines around 1900.

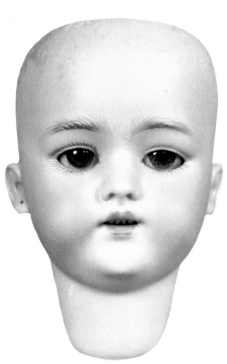

Swivel-head doll. Neck extends into the body and fastens from within, so head can be turned.

Doll Bodies

Body Combinations

Many materials were used to make bodies for porcelain, parian and bisque dolls. These materials included porcelain, wood, fabric, composition, papier-mâché and leather. They were combined with other materials, so fabric or leather bodies might have arms and legs of wood or porcelain.

Wood Bodies

Wood dolls were made before porcelain was discovered. Later, porcelain and bisque heads were combined with wood bodies. Wood dolls and bodies were made in many places, especially Gröden, the Grödner Valley and South Tyrol. By 1810, eight-jointed wood bodies were being made. Two Grödner dolls with bisque heads and jointed wood bodies are shown on page 143.

Composition

Pulp is the fiber mash left after paper is made. It was added to different substances for easy shaping. Pulp was later improved by adding substances, such as clay, sand and chalk, and the resulting product was called *composition*. Many bisque heads had composition bodies.

Composition and wood-composition bodies were the most common for dolls with bisque heads. Bodies had 8 to 10 joints, which made them flexible. The swivel-jointed head was first made in 1861 and patented in 1869 by French doll maker, Casimir Bru.

The ball-and-socket jointed body was first made by Heinrich Stier in 1880. Joints could move forward and sideways through the use of a socket-linked ball joint. Joints were usually made of wood, bodies were made of composition and arms were often made of wood. These bodies are called *wood-composition*.

Smaller dolls were fashionable. Knees of toddler doll bodies, which were short and stocky, were shifted so the unsightly ball joint was no longer visible.

Stiff-limbed bodies, introduced by 1890, were a step backward with regard to movement. This type of body had only four joints.

In 1909, sitting babies with bent limbs modeled after a 6-month-old human baby became popular. These dolls could only sit. Standing babies, modeled after a 2-year-old child, were registered in 1912. They had immovable knees and could stand. Standing-and-sitting baby dolls could fulfill both functions.

Papier-Mâché

The predecessor of papier-mâché was pulp, which achieved stability through pasting together many layers of cardboard. Pulp was stiff and

Bisque, marked *Ruth.*
Shoulder-head doll with leather body and wired joints. In most cases, body was made of kidskin, sheep leather or waxed fabric. Arms were usually porcelain or Celluloid.

difficult to shape. Later, thinner layers of pulp were softened in paste water, pressed into a half mold and individual layers were glued with adhesive. Moist, dry half pieces were removed from the molds, dried and bound together with glue.

During the softening process, pulp became moldable and was called *papier-mâché*. At first it was prepared by hand, then later it was made mechanically. Papier-mâché dolls could be made in stamping machines.

Papier-mâché becomes stable when dried and forced into hollow shapes for heads and limbs. Hollow fingers cannot be made. They must be cast thicker, and often fingers are broken.

Cloth or Leather Bodies

A doll's cloth or leather body was sewn together, then filled with various materials, such as sawdust, horsehair, cotton wool or seaweed. Cloth and leather casings were sewn or pasted on shoulderplates. For leather bodies, kid and sheep leather were preferred, although these materials were replaced by imitation leather after 1900.

On inexpensive German dolls, limbs were often merely sewn on. On some more-expensive German and French dolls, bodies were sewn with gussets, which made better movement of the doll possible.

Leather bodies made with joints were fastened together in various ways. Inside the bodies were wire bindings, which were riveted and sewn, joints and other devices. Too many variations of bodies, joints and limbs proved to be the doll makers' downfall.

All-Bisque Dolls

Dolls made completely from bisque are called *all-bisque*. One example is the little doll sitting at the well on page 48. Her head is immobile and firmly attached to her body. Bath dolls are also considered all-bisque. Most were made of china, but a few were made of bisque.

Small bath dolls were called *Frozen Charlottes* and *Frozen Charlies*. Blond dolls are rarer than dark ones. Knickknack dolls made of china or bisque, such as those on page 147, are considered all-bisque.

Doll Bodies and Their Conditions

To judge the original condition and value of a doll, you must look at the head and condition of the clothes. The condition of the body is also important.

If a doll served its original purpose, it was played with. Through playing, a finger might be broken or the head damaged. If possible, undress a doll before you buy it. You will be able to see if it has a repaired head or an acquired head, which in its size, characteristics, markings or period is not correct for the doll.

Bisque, Handwerck and Simon & Halbig, marked *Heinrich Handwerck, Simon & Halbig.* Classic German ball-jointed composition doll with 12 joints, shaped torso, strongly molded hands and swivel head.

Doll Clothes

Dolls with porcelain heads are 80 to 100 years old, and in some cases, over 120 years old. Often, little remains of original clothes, as photos on this and the opposite page show. Time, wear and tear cause deterioration. Not many dolls were kept in display cases or protected from moths and other causes of damage.

It is not often an old doll is found in good condition in original clothing. When they are found, these dolls may demand a higher price, up to 30% above normal value.

Frequently, a doll is found in its second or third change of clothes. This is acceptable if old materials were used and if the cut and style are similar to the style of the time. These criteria should guide you if you re-dress your doll.

Costuming is a wonderful hobby and at the same time it makes a doll more beautiful. That means joy for collectors and those who view collections.

At flea markets, second-hand stores, in great-grandmother's closet and whenever the opportunity presents itself, search for old fabrics, lace, ribbon and flowers. You may find rich rewards that will give you many years of pleasure.

Costuming dolls demands good taste, fine sewing and correct use of styles and materials. Old catalogs, fashion magazines and photographs can serve as patterns for costumes, such as those shown on pages 24 and 25. For additional information on costuming, see *Doll Costuming*, by Mildred and Colleen Seeley, also published by HPBooks. It deals with making costumes for German and French bisque dolls.

German dolls were not dressed as elegantly or expensively as French ones. They were often sold wearing only a slip or chemise. If a doll is offered for sale in this condition, it is probably in its original costume. But this half-naked state is not original clothing in the conventional sense.

A children's book from 1890 shows dolls dressed by the loving, hard-working hands of mothers and grandmothers. Home-dressed dolls were often beautifully costumed.

In many families, it was customary for a doll to be newly dressed on Christmas or a child's birthday. Favorites often had wardrobes, called *trousseaus*, which included accessories such as fans, hats, handbags and other necessary items.

Doll play permitted a great deal of variety. For this reason, in 1910 Kestner released the *Wonder Doll* with two exchangable heads and wigs. Kämmer & Reinhardt later made a doll with three heads.

Because French dolls were dressed more elegantly than German ones, German dolls often wore French clothes. In the interest of authenticity, do not put French clothes on a German doll. It is immediately noticeable.

Bru and Jumeau dolls wore particular clothing styles. French costumes were made of expensive materials and decorated with pleats and frills. Bodices had inserts of tied lace or silk. Collars were large or small, pointed or round. Hats and bonnets were beautiful with frills, bows, flowers, feathers and veils.

Clothes of silk, such as those shown above, bring no higher price than cotton clothes. This costume shows what can happen if collectors do not attempt to preserve dolls and their clothes.

Doll's silk costume has deteriorated.

Maker unknown

Bisque, possibly Simon & Halbig, 21-3/4 inches (55cm), *marked 79 DEP 5*. Shoulder-head doll is tinted bisque with pink cheeks. Blue glass sleep eyes have fiber irises, black-hair upper eyelashes, painted lower eyelashes and painted eyebrows. Slightly open bow mouth has four teeth. Doll wears original ash-blond mohair wig. Leather body has cut leather fingers. Clothes are original.

Original doll dress form,
13-3/4 inches (35cm) high

Cast-iron, hand-cranked
sewing machine for children
made in 1890 works and is 6
inches (15cm) wide

Steam iron, 1-3/4 inches (4cm) long

Doll corset from the 20th century

Illustration from *New Dressing Dolls*, 1880. Drawings and printed patterns for making clothes at home were available in fashion magazines. Doll clothes were often in the style of children's clothing.

No. 8567. Neu-Ruppin, zu haben bei Gustav Kühn

From book titled *The Little Doll Mother's School of Embroidery.*

Dressmaker's pattern sheet 1.
In 1890, *The Little Doll Mother's School of Embroidery*
included information about sewing doll clothes. It
contained directions and patterns for making many
different garments.

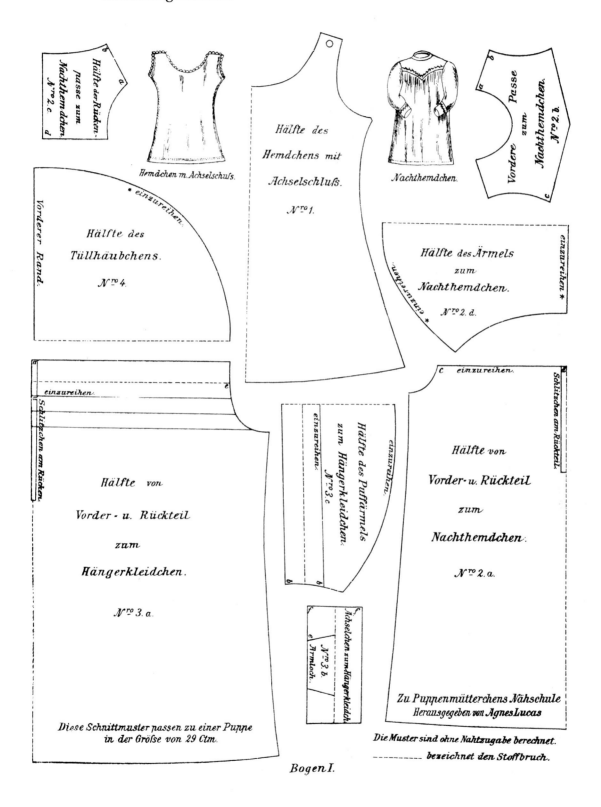

Bogen I.

Doll hats were designed in the fashion of the times. Victorian bonnets, caps and straw hats were popular, and colorful bows, flowers and lace added decoration. Doll hat shops were similar to real stores and had many beautiful hats.

Showcase above displays several beautiful old doll hats. In middle of upper row is original Jumeau hat. At center bottom is a sun hat on its original hatbox.

Pictures on opposite page illustrate different hat fashions.

Alt, Beck & Gottschalk of Thuringia, established in 1845. Company made bath dolls, porcelain dolls, bisque heads and dolls.

A.C.J. Anger of Aich bei Bohemia, successor of Moehling porcelain factory, established in 1900. Company made bisque heads. A&M mark is frequently confused with AM, the mark for Armand Marseille.

Carl Bergner of Thuringia, established in 1860. Company made bisque dolls and baby dolls.

Cuno and Otto Dressel of Thuringia, established in 1700. Company made many different doll bodies and used doll heads by Simon & Halbig and Armand Marseille.

Heinrich Handwerck of Thuringia, established in 1876. Company made jointed, character and baby dolls. Used many bisque heads from Simon & Halbig.

Max Handwerck of Thuringia, established in 1900. Company made character dolls and jointed baby dolls.

German Doll Makers

Heinrich Handwerck

The Heinrich Handwerck Co. was located in Waltershausen. It was formed in 1876 and distinguished itself early as the maker of ball-jointed dolls. In 1893, it received the highest distinction for this development at the World's Fair in Chicago.

By 1902, the firm was taken over by Kämmer & Reinhardt, but retained its previous name. The Handwerck firm had been linked with their *Bébé Cosmopolite*, made in 1895, and their *Bébé Reclamé*, made in 1898. These dolls solidified their reputation. In 1913, *Bébé Superior* was introduced.

Handwerck dolls represented novelties and were associated with technical improvements. They had bisque heads with sleep eyes, open mouths with teeth and mohair wigs. Bodies had ball joints at the neck, shoulders, elbows, wrists, hips and knees. Heads of Handwerck dolls were made by Simon & Halbig, but the label read *Handwerck's*.

After 1910, Handwerck began making character dolls with joints. They were designed after living models by artists from Munich. In 1912, boy and girl dolls were produced. They were dressed in native costumes or Oriental kimonos.

Character baby dolls followed in 1914. In 1921, Handwerck's son broke away from Kämmer & Reinhardt and brought the firm under family management again. Production was enhanced in 1925 with dolls that could move their eyes sideways. The first dolls with sleep eyes were made in 1927.

Heubach Brothers

Christoph and Philipp Heubach from Thuringia established a doll workshop in 1820. They put together dolls and used cloth bodies made by other companies. By 1840, the Heubachs had acquired a porcelain factory and began producing doll heads and limbs.

But only after 1882 can heads with their signature be found. They introduced trademark *Sonne am Horizont*, which means sun on the horizon. In 1894, 400 workers were employed by the brothers, which by then numbered three.

After 1891, signing heads became almost mandatory, and Heubach dolls are reliably marked. The majority of the delicate, pink-bisque ones have model numbers printed in green.

By 1911, the firm had become a family corporation. It commissioned well-known contemporary artists to design character doll heads. Heads with closed mouths, painted eyes and hair are famous. There were often two versions of the same doll.

One child doll was called *Einco*. It had large eyes, a round face, a closed mouth and wore a skirt and wool cloak. It was one of the most impressive Heubach child dolls. Its face appears expressionless. It is rare today.

Another Heubach doll was called *Pfeifer*. Its lips are so pursed, it looks as if it is whistling. The doll can make a pipe sound if a knob on the body is pressed.

Other character dolls made by Heubach include one with an angry face and a baby that looks real, but wears a toddler hat. The doll was made of fragile bisque and is difficult to find.

8192
Germany
Gebrüder Heubach

Heubach Brothers of Thuringia, established in 1820. Company made porcelain and bisque dolls.

Heubach-Köppelsdorf
Germany

Ernst Heubach of Köppelsdorf, established in 1885. Company made bisque doll heads with open nostrils and dolls with roguish eyes.

Bisque, Kämmer & Reinhardt, 15-3/4 inches (40cm).
Made around 1918, character doll has painted gray eyes and wears uniform of a medical orderly.

Kämmer & Reinhardt of Thuringia, established in 1866. Company held many patents and was major manufacturer of character dolls and baby dolls. Used bisque heads from Simon & Halbig. K(star)R is one of company's most recognizable markings. Two typical K(star)R marks are shown above.

Because of their artfully designed heads, in contrast to simply constructed heads, Heubach dolls are expensive to purchase. Many owners use them as *piano dolls*, which are placed out of danger on the piano, because they are beautiful and easily broken.

Another firm named Heubach made dolls and was located in Köppelsdorf. Their dolls had little in common with those made by the Heubach Brothers of Thuringia. Dolls of the Heubachs of Köppelsdorf lacked individuality, which was the signature of the Thuringia dolls. Snub noses and laughing mouths are traits of the dolls of Köppelsdorf, but they are not the same quality as those of Thuringia.

Kämmer & Reinhardt

Kämmer & Reinhardt began making dolls in 1886 in Waltershausen. They made some of the most beautiful German dolls. *K&R* was a well-known trademark in the business by 1895. Designs were done by one of the partners—Ernst Kämmer—who created and made many beautiful dolls.

From the company's beginning, it was their motto "to walk no trampled paths, but always create something new, distinguished as a first class article." When Ernst Kämmer died in 1901, Karl Krauser took over the artistic direction of the company. He made new, interesting dolls.

Within five years, a new project grew from a small operation. Kämmer & Reinhardt obtained heads from Simon & Halbig because they produced beautiful bisque. Together, the two companies produced high-quality bodies.

In 1909, the Kämmer & Reinhardt company began producing character dolls. The baby of the series is considered valuable today, as are Hansel and Gretel dolls produced in 1909. A number on the head gives the size. From this, we can determine whether the head and body came from the same manufacturer.

The 1927 Kämmer & Reinhardt catalog showed a large variety of child dolls with traditional curls and pageboy haircuts. Most character dolls are signed and named. Doll No.101 was named Peter and Marie. No.114 was a pouty-mouth doll called Hans and Gretchen. No.126 became the most widely known character doll of this class.

The firm of Handwerck was merged with Kämmer & Reinhardt from 1902 to 1921. The child doll heads they made, in conjunction with Simon & Halbig's beautiful bisque, contributed to the fame and popularity of the K&R dolls and helped establish their solid reputation.

J.D. Kestner, Jr.

The Kestner firm was founded in 1805 in Waltershaus, where the company made the crown doll. Johann Daniel Kestner, later court agent and counsel to the Duke of Saxony, was the first toy maker to travel with samples of his collection to exhibit at Leipzig. The firm displayed there regularly beginning in 1840. In 1867, this exhibit was taken over by Johann's uncle, Adolf Kestner.

The *Junior* in the firm name dates from 1836. After 1836, the company made dolls with porcelain heads and limbs. These were made in a porcelain factory incorporated by the firm in Ohrdruf.

Bodies were leather bags with gussets for flexibility. Heads are character heads, distinguished by hollow cheeks and open-closed mouths with teeth.

Beginning in 1860, the firm made bisque heads and bodies. It was the

**Bisque, Kestner, neck mark JDK
214.**
This doll was made around 1910.

K &⟨✡⟩ *R*

SIMON & HALBIG
717W

Mark commonly used for dolls from
Kämmer & Reinhardt with heads by
Simon & Halbig.

J.D.K.

made in
Germany
B5

J.D. Kestner, Jr. of Thuringia,
established in 1805. Company made
bisque dolls.

only firm in Germany to produce doll heads and bodies. They assembled
dolls from parts in bulk lots and sold them as original. The firm's identity
mark, *J.D.K.*, is often missing on its dolls. Instead, dolls were marked
with letters, the label *Germany*, and the number of the head size.

The firm assigned letters of the *Kestner alphabet* to identify doll types.
Baby dolls carried manufacturer's numbers exclusively. Serialized
babies are recognizable by their first names. For example, one baby with
painted hair is labeled *Hilda J.D.K.* The Googly is especially sought after
today. Kestner also made Kewpie dolls, copied after American models.

Kestner's Oriental doll carries No.243 and is valuable to today's
collectors. It is preferred over the Oriental doll of Armand Marseille.
The almond-shape eyes and its flat, molded face are still beautiful.

The company staff numbered 1164 in 1845. The birthplace of its
founder, Court Counselor Kestner, had to be taken over for use in
making dolls. The firm was famous for its high-quality products and for
the beautiful facial expressions of its dolls.

Armand Marseille

The French name is misleading—Armand Marseille was one of the
most-famous Thuringian doll makers of the 19th century. He was born
in St. Petersburg and was the son of a Huguenot elder. He had time and
money, so he could seek a profession in peace. After traveling through
Europe, he was attracted by the Sonneberg toy industry.

He went to Sonneberg, where he started a toy factory in 1884. A year
later, he bought a porcelain factory that made pitchers and pipe bowls.

In 1886, Marseille merged with the Heubach Brothers, which also
made dolls. After 1919, the firm was called the *United Köppelsdorf Porcelain Factory*. The Marseille and Heubach families grew together both in
and out of business. Marseille's son Herman married Beatrix, the daughter of Ernst Heubach.

In 1890, after years of experimenting, Marseille began producing
bisque doll heads. The business flourished and employed 550 workers.
The company produced porcelain heads exclusively.

Almost all Marseille dolls are marked with *A.M.* or the full name of
Armand Marseille. Only a few can be found with neck marks of other
makers. The quality of Marseille heads was so high, they were in great
demand in France and America.

Because of mass production, Armand Marseille dolls are fairly easy to
find and are reasonably priced. They are more attractive than dolls of
simpler construction.

The most-common model was doll No.390. She looks like an illustration from a 19th century children's book, with her delicate, softly molded
face. Dolls with head No.370 have a shoulder attachment and can be
found with either inexpensive or beautifully worked bodies. Bodies
were covered with leather and riveted with slightly movable joints.

Armand Marseille made inexpensive dolls and expensive character
dolls. Those made entirely by Marseille are fairly rare. The same porcelain head model was often combined with many bodies. The prototype,
No.500, is a boy with an almost-imperceptible smile. His head was combined with many bodies.

Marseille baby dolls were more realistic than others. No.640 was a girl
with engraved eyes and a sweet smile. Baby Betty, No.390, was first produced in 1894. She differs from other child dolls because her brown color
looks similar to an Indian doll. Colored baby dolls were usually sleep
dolls with open or closed mouths. They looked foreign only because of
their coloring.

K & H
Germany

Kley & Hahn of Thuringia, established in 1895. Company made bath dolls, china, parian and bisque heads, character babies and dolls. Owned trademark for *Walkuere* (Valkyrie), *Schneewittchen* (Snow White) and *Meine Einzige* (My Only One).

Armand Marseille
Germany
390
A 11/0 M

Armand Marseille of Thuringia, established in 1865. Company made bisque dolls.

Revalo
8½

Ohlhaver Brothers of Thuringia, established in 1912. Company made ball-jointed dolls and baby dolls with bisque heads. Used three marks: *Revalo, My Queen Doll* and *Bébé Princesse.*

S 8H
SH 1079-12
DEP
S 11 K
949
SIMON & HALBIG

Simon & Halbig of Thuringia, established in 1870. Company made bisque shoulder-head dolls and heads. Supplied heads to many doll makers and held many patents. Four typical marks are shown above.

S PB H
1909
6
Germany

Schoenau & Hoffmeister of Oberfr, established in 1901. Company made dolls and bisque heads. *SH* is frequently confused with Simon & Halbig. *PB* in star stands for *Porzellanfabrik Burggrub.*

Simon & Halbig

The Simon & Halbig Co. of Thuringia was founded in 1869 as a porcelain manufacturer. One partner, Wilhelm Simon, was co-owner of the Simon & Co. toy factory in Hildburghausen, which made doll bodies. Doll hands were made by the Halbig firm. The large demand for toy dolls made a factory necessary.

Simon found a partner in the porcelain maker, Halbig, and the firm of Simon & Halbig came into being. Dolls were produced by Halbig and assembled by Simon.

In 1870, heads of tinted bisque were made by Halbig and put on fabric or leather bodies made by Simon. Dolls became more realistic around 1880, when painted hair was replaced by wigs and inset glass eyes were used.

Many dolls were made and sent to France. Only unmarked ones were offered for sale in other countries. The quality was the same, and these bisque dolls, as delicately molded as the French ones, won the foreign market. The lightly tinted torso, molded breast and beautiful head were adapted to the French *petites enfants.*

After joining with Kämmer & Reinhardt, Simon & Halbig was commissioned to make character dolls. Only a few carry the label of Simon & Halbig.

Many experiments were done with facial expressions. To spur the market, colored dolls were made about the turn of the century. Negro, Indian and Chinese dolls were popular during this period. Character dolls became more popular after 1900. The number *1448* signifies a character doll with a winning smile, and today she is rare. Sleep eyes and a closed mouth give her special charm.

Doll No.1388 is exceptional. She has a hinged mouth, molded teeth and a facial expression that could almost be adult. This does not fit the concept of other dolls. Doll No.153 has painted eyes and molded, light hair. Doll No.1358 is a Negro child with a closed mouth, sleep eyes and pierced ears.

Maker Unknown

Dolls by unknown makers may be more beautiful and valuable. See page 56. Often they carry numbers, letters or the labels *Germany* or *Made in Germany.* The phrase *Made in Germany* appeared after the English trade laws of 1887. These laws required a declaration of the country of origin to appear on things exported to England. The label *DRGM* stands for *Deutsches Reichs-gebrauchsmuster* or German patent. *Dep* stands for *deponiert als Gebrauchs-und Geschmacksmuster*, which means "certified as patented and meeting standards of good taste."

Sorting and classifying eyes

Waltershausen,
the Homeland of Dolls

Report written in 1888 by A. Trinius, published in *Illustrierte Welt (Illustrated World)*.

Many people in the forests of Thuringia are involved in making dolls. To the south, villages cluster around the flourishing town of Sonneberg. At the other end of the mountain range in the forests of the northern slope, people do handwork for companies in Waltershausen. Sonneberg and Waltershausen share the honor of supplying the world with dolls. Sonneberg has made more dolls, but Waltershausen produces an equal product. For inventiveness, Waltershausen is the premier city. They have accomplished a gradual growth by starting new factories.

Doll painters and artists

Old, young, big, small, men, women—all are hard at work with dolls. Factories of both cities are used to assemble the dolls. Individual parts flow into these factories from all over the country. Many people who live in villages carve arms or legs, shape heads or bodies or turn ball joints on lathes. This goes on from morning till night in house after house. At the end of the school day, children help out. There are bodies to stuff and sew up, often for only a few cents per dozen. When everyone helps, they assemble and work together.

Where painters live, racks of freshly painted doll heads are seen in windows of houses and along garden fences. One painter is a master painter and specializes in lips and dimples. Another has learned to paint eyes and arching brows. A row of other painters dip individual limbs into flesh-color glue. On Saturday morning, everything is loaded on wheelbarrows and taken to the city to sell.

Doll-making workshop in Finsterbergen

Often people in the city are involved. In addition to factory work, home industries prosper. If you wander through the alleys and glance through the uncurtained windows of apartments, you will see artists and painters.

Women and girls work with their skilled hands giving shape to the long, wavy hair of the dolls. Style is important—many child workers wear their hair in the fashion their factory has chosen for the year's standard. One can determine from hairstyles which firms the children work for.

Once a doll is assembled, varnished, painted and coiffed, it goes to be costumed and packed, and the cottage industries play their role. One family makes shiny shoes. Another sews dainty dresses. In one place, boxes are pasted together. In another, the doll is wrapped with blue ribbon and placed in its box. Boxes are placed in massive crates lined with sheet metal, and crates are put in the hands of the delivery men.

Sonneberg, Doll City of Thuringia

Report published in 1895 in *Illustrierte Welt (Illustrated World)*.

I am a "lucky" person. My son once filled my gold seven-day watch with water. For this deed, he was hailed by my wife as a profound philosopher and great experimenter. I have a lovable dachshund that dislikes mailmen intensely. The mailman has handed me many bills for hosiery. I have three daughters—Annie, Lisa and Kitty—who shatter doll heads on sofa legs and tear the legs off their bath babies.

The girls appeared before me in single file one Sunday morning, all freshly washed and dressed. Each held out a torn-off doll arm, saying "Look, Papa, look!" I was enraged, and I swore the doll question had been settled once and for all. My wife countered with her friendly smile. "Why the excitement, dear? Children always do things like this. And I think it is darling that they did it as a surprise for you!"

This added fuel to the fire. I defended my conclusions with strong arguments and a stronger voice. She finally said to me sharply, "All right, all right! Have it your way, and don't bring your poor children anything from your trips, especially dolls!"

I rewarded her with a dark, threatening glare, and she cried.

I am a man of my word, and my decisions are final. I went off on my next trip, gloomy and grim. What I left behind me was an armed truce in my family. My wife's last words were "Please, no dolls!" and her lip quivered in grief.

"That is really not necessary, I swear . . ." My wife quickly shushed me. Because I am sentimental when leaving for a trip, I tenderly kissed her little hand. But my resolve was not shaken in any way!

My locomotive puffed its way through Thuringia. Next to me in the coach sat a fat, pleasant man. The conductor came to our window. "Tickets to Sonneberg?"

My neighbor cleared his throat and said, with a glance at my wedding ring and careworn brow, "That is the doll city!" I asked for further explanation. He was a businessman who was interested in numbers. According to him, Sonneberg was a city with over 12,000 inhabitants that exported 15 million dolls and toys that went to all the world as Nuremberg toys. Nuremburg toys were made in Sonneberg. The woodworking industry prospered, even during the 30 Years' War.

"Here you can study the social ladder of the doll world, from 50 pfennigs per dozen to 100 marks per doll. There is class hatred and prejudice. Penny dolls seem more oppressed than grand lady dolls. Last year I took my niece with me to our country retreat, and she had only one wish—to live and die in Sonneberg."

I responded that an irrevocable house rule, to which I was bound by sacred oaths, forbade me from buying dolls. He said he considered such house rules had the same purpose as many other laws. They were made to be broken!

This revealed him as a leftist liberal, and I am a conservative. Our debate became heated and energetic while the train puffed on. He proposed class order be overthrown in the doll world. I resolved to prove the contrary.

Varnishing parts of doll bodies

Preparing and assembling parts of jointed dolls

Cutting and sewing doll bodies

We got off the train as he gave me an overview of the doll and toy industry. There were cottage industries, each having its particular specialty. Before we got to the expense of the export industry, we visited many houses to evaluate the various phases of doll making.

First he led me to a doll-body maker. There sat father and son with a pot of sawdust. They stuffed the doll bodies with incredible speed. At another table, the daughter glued arm and leg pieces to the limbs and sewed them together.

We next walked behind a giant crate of doll legs and torsos to the neighboring presser. He finished gray paper-pulp heads and lived in steamy temperatures.

I studied glass eyes when we went to the neighboring town of Lauscha. The factory produced them in great numbers and supplied the world with set eyes and sleep eyes.

Next, we saw how heads were painted. Each head was treated as colorfast. One person painted the head, and a second cut out glued-up eye holes with a sharp blade. A third painted lips a brilliant red and painted eyebrows.

This was all done with accuracy and symmetry because of years of practice. Next the head and scalp were glued together and a wig of mohair was added. Hairs of wax dolls were placed in the wax individually.

Heads showed great diversity. Wood, paper pulp, china, bisque and wax were used. Better dolls had a charming elegance of workmanship.

Clothing was fitted in the final stages. Dozens of shops were engaged in this business alone. Dolls were dressed as a simple village maid, a woman of society, children and stylish cavalry lieutenants.

"And here," said my guide, as he led me into a brightly lit warehouse, "is the splendor of this nation of toys, and I am the king of the realm." He cordially invited me to take a fine specimen of a lady doll, along with two simpler sisters. "That is, if your house rules . . ."

I turned red and tried to refuse. But one cannot overrule a king in his own realm.

Washing heads

Attaching hair

Stuffing doll bodies

Doll hairdressers

Character Dolls

Character dolls are lifelike representations of real people, especially children and babies. The term was first used by the firm of Kämmer & Reinhardt in 1909 after they had achieved success with dolls named *My Darling* or *The Flirt*.

The idea of making dolls that looked similar to real people originated with a group of Munich artists. In the summer of 1908, the group introduced a doll, called the *Munich Art Doll*, that made history. The purpose of the group was to get away from stereotyped, idealized dolls.

Although Kämmer & Reinhardt regarded artists' dolls as offensive, they were motivated by them to bring their own ideas to fruition. They employed an artist from Berlin who introduced a bronze bust he had sculptured of a 6-week-old baby. At first regarded as too realistic and ugly, they hesitated before introducing it as a baby doll in 1909, called *Kaiser baby*, No.100. See page 133. It became a success, and Kämmer & Reinhardt could hardly meet the demand.

Character dolls were a breakthrough, and the incentive for new achievements was born. Shortly after, a group of Berlin artists designed the successful *Peter* and *Marie* dolls, No.101.

The pattern-maker for Kämmer & Reinhardt was commissioned to design a new doll from a living model—the grandson of Franz Reinhardt. It went into production as No.114 in 1910 under the names of *Hans* and *Gretchen*. They are the same doll, and differ only in their wigs and clothing. They were loved and desired in 1910, and this is still true today. Their popularity was due to the beautiful, molded, slightly bow mouth, called a *pouty mouth*.

If all these dolls had been introduced with sleep eyes, such as the later No.117A doll, see page 107, from Kämmer & Reinhardt and Simon & Halbig, their commercial success would have been greater.

Other German doll makers used the same idea and began making character dolls. Among these were the firms of Heinrich Handwerck, the Heubach Brothers, Kestner, Marseille, Kley & Hahn and Simon & Halbig. Character-doll makers always oriented themselves to certain standards of beauty, but integrated reality into their newer creations.

More lifelike child dolls were produced. Simon & Halbig's No.1448, shown on pages 110 and 111, is a beautiful doll that is almost unattainable by collectors. Apparently only a trial series of 100 pieces was made.

Kämmer & Reinhardt's beautiful No.117, with head by Simon & Halbig, marks the high point of German doll design.

In 1924, Armand Marseille named his No.341 and No.351 character baby, *My Dream Baby*. See pages 127 and 135. The No.341 doll had a closed mouth, and No.351 had an open mouth. Kley & Hahn gave some of their character dolls names such as *Valkyrie*, *Snow White* and *My Very Own*.

Before leaving character dolls, we must mention Googlies, page 117. Googlies were made by almost all the large firms and were popular then, as they are today.

Bisque, Kämmer & Reinhardt, 9-1/2 inches (24cm), marked *K(star)R114*. Character doll, named *Gretchen*, made around 1914, has a ball-jointed, composition body.

Bisque, Kämmer & Reinhardt, Simon & Halbig. Character doll with little sister. Both dolls from K(star)R 117A series.

China-Head Dolls

Glazed porcelain, which was used to make *china-head* dolls, was rediscovered by doll makers in 1845. China-head dolls were not popular because they were cold, white and had an unpleasant shine. Many china heads were dressed in the style of the late Victorian Era, and their molded hair or wigs were suited to that period. China-head dolls with cloth bodies were called *Nanking dolls.*

Small Victorian wicker basket lined with cloth, made around 1860.

Maker unknown

China, maker unknown, 14-1/2 inches (37cm). Made around 1875, shoulder-head doll is china head with strongly tinted pink cheeks. Painted blue eyes have lid streaks and black eyebrows. Closed mouth has red midline, and ears have an opening. Hair is black and molded. Stuffed body has porcelain forearms and lower legs. Clothes are original.

Balanced swivel mirror of lathe-turned
walnut wood, made in 1880, is 7 inches
(18cm) high.

Maker unknown

China, maker unknown, doll on left is 11 inches (28cm),
doll on right is 9-3/4 inches (25cm). Brother and sister dolls
made around 1890 have pink cheeks, painted blue eyes
and painted eyebrows. Mouths are closed. Doll on left has
blond molded, painted hair, and doll on right has black
molded, painted hair. Fabric bodies were restored by hand,
and arms are porcelain. New clothes are made of old fabric.

Bronze wrought-iron bed, made around 1900, is 11-3/4x19-3/4 inches
(30x50cm). Doll is shown on opposite page with hair up, wearing necklace, and
is described below.

Maker unknown

China, maker unknown, 22-3/4 inches (58cm). Made
around 1870, shoulder-head doll is china with pink-tinted
cheeks. Painted blue eyes have red lid streaks and painted
eyebrows. Mouth is closed, and ears are pierced. Doll
wears original, hand-tied human-hair wig. Leather body
has leather arms and separately sewn fingers. Clothes, lace
stockings and shoes are old.

China and Parian Bath Dolls

Bath dolls first appeared around 1860. They were made of china or parian and were white or tinted pink. Bath dolls had a hole in the back of the body or head, and they were favorite bath toys of children. Closed fists were a common feature of bath dolls. Dolls were designed to stand upright, but some sitting bath dolls were made. Smaller girl and boy dolls were called *Frozen Charlotte* and *Frozen Charlie* dolls.

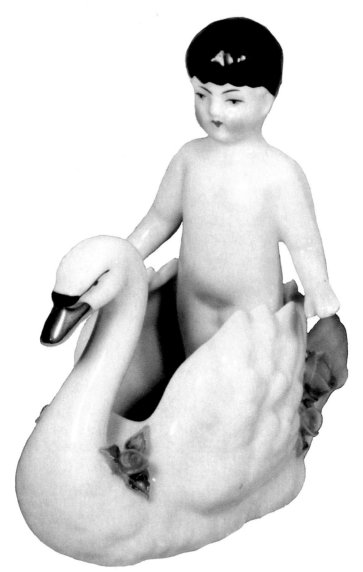

Doll in china swan is described below.

Maker unknown

China, maker unknown, doll on left is 5 inches (13cm), doll on right is 5-1/2 inches (14cm), doll in tub is miniature. Doll with blond premolded hair was made around 1900 and has closed fists. Doll with black hair was made around 1910 and has painted hair and open hands with palms turned down. In the tub is a miniature bath doll, called a *Frozen Charlotte*. All three dolls have red-tinted cheeks, painted eyes and eyebrows, and painted mouths.

Parian Dolls

Parian is a white, mat porcelain, named after Parian marble. It was introduced in 1842 by the Copeland Company in England. Parian was made from silica, clay, chalk, soda, magnesia and other elements. Parian dolls had molded painted hair, molded ornaments, molded painted hats and molded stockings and shoes. These dolls were popular for a short time and were replaced by bisque dolls.

Hand-decorated Victorian pearl purse made around 1880.

Maker unknown

Parian, maker unknown, 11-3/4 inches (30cm). Made around 1880, this doll was called a *bonnet doll*. Eyes are painted, body is stuffed and arms and legs are porcelain. Molded bonnet is late-Victorian style. Doll wears molded pink garters and molded green high-button boots with heels.

Dolls in the Victorian Style

Often dolls are referred to as *Victorian*, even though they were not made during the Victorian period. When bisque appeared in 1860, special bisque dolls were made that displayed typical Victorian attributes, such as hairstyles, clothes and accessories. It is acceptable to speak of these dolls as "Victorian style" and to classify them this way for collectors.

Iron bed with velvet canopy and embroidered curtains, made around 1880, is 19-3/4x17-3/4 inches (50x45cm). Doll is shown in close-up photo on opposite page and is described below.

Maker unknown

Bisque, maker unknown, 16-1/2 inches (42cm). Made around 1870, turned-head doll has molded blond curls. Painted blue eyes have red lid streaks and painted eyebrows. Small closed mouth has red midline. Cloth body has bisque lower legs and forearms. Clothes are old silk and lace.

Bisque Shoulder-Head Dolls

Shoulder-head dolls have head, neck and shoulders made in one piece. Turned-head dolls have the head, neck and shoulders made in one piece, but the head is molded so it is slightly tilted or turned to one side. The head does not move. Bisque was mat and painted after the first firing, then fired again.

Pump fountain made around 1920. Small all-bisque doll sitting on fountain is made of tinted bisque. She has molded blond hair, painted brown eyes and red cheeks. She wears molded, painted stockings and shoes. Larger doll is shown in close-up photo on opposite page and is described below.

Dressel

Bisque, Dressel, 16-1/2 inches (42cm), marked *dep D/7*. Made around 1890, turned-head doll is tinted bisque, with brown-pink tinted cheeks and dimples. Fixed, blue glass eyes have rayed irises, painted eyelashes and painted eyebrows. Open mouth has tinted lips. Doll wears original human-hair wig. Body is shaped fabric, and arms, hands and lower legs are composition. New costume is made of old fabric.

Fan made around 1875 is 6 inches (15cm) high.

Kestner

Bisque, Kestner, Jr., 26-3/4 inches (68cm), marked *M. Made in Germany*. Made around 1875, turned-head doll is pink-tinted bisque. Fixed, gray-blue glass eyes have rayed irises, painted eyelashes and painted eyebrows. Mouth is closed, with emphasized lines, and cheeks have dimples. Doll wears original human-hair wig. Leather body has four joints, with six-jointed composition arms. New costume is made of old English linen, old lace and an old child's bonnet.

Dolls are shown together in photo on opposite page.

Armand Marseille

Bisque, Armand Marseille, 22-3/4 inches (58cm), marked *370 AM 5. DEP made in Germany.* Made around 1900, turned-head doll is pink-tinted bisque with orange-pink cheeks. Dark-blue sleep eyes have rayed irises, painted eyelashes and deeply molded, dark-brown eyebrows. Colored bow mouth is slightly open with four teeth on top. Doll wears new mohair wig. Old cloth body has molded porcelain arms. Clothes are old.

Armand Marseille

Bisque, Armand Marseille, 25-1/2 inches (65cm), marked *370 AM 7. DEP.* Made around 1900, shoulder-head doll is pink-tinted bisque with pink cheeks. Brown glass sleep eyes have painted eyelashes and painted eyebrows. Slightly open mouth has four teeth. Doll wears hand-tied human-hair wig. Original brown leather body has restored Celluloid arms. New costume is made of old fabric.

Dolls photographed with balloons. Left: Alt, Beck and Gottschalk doll is described on page 73. Right: Armand Marseille 370 doll is shown in close-up photo on opposite page and is described below.

Armand Marseille

Bisque, Armand Marseille, 19 inches (48cm), marked *370 DEP A.M.* Made around 1900, turned-head doll is clear pink-tinted bisque with pink cheeks. Gray-blue glass sleep eyes have painted eyelashes and painted brown eyebrows. Open mouth has four teeth on top. Doll wears original human-hair wig. Leather body has cloth lower legs and beautifully shaped porcelain hands. New clothes are made of old fabrics.

Maker unknown

Bisque, maker unknown, 24-1/2 inches (62cm). Made around 1885, doll has a molded bust. Bisque is fair, with tinted orange-red cheeks. Blue glass sleep eyes have rayed irises, painted eyelashes and tinted, plumed eyebrows. Mouth is closed. Doll wears original hand-tied human-hair wig. Old cloth body has restored arms. New costume is made of old material. There is an old photograph in the brooch.

Maker unknown

Bisque, probably Kestner, 15-3/4 inches (40cm). Made
around 1890, turned-head doll has pink-tinted cheeks.
Fixed, sky-blue eyes have rayed irises, painted eyelashes
and painted feathery eyebrows. Mouth is closed. Doll
wears original blond-mohair wig. Leather body has shaped
arms and bisque hands. Original clothes are decorated
with antique lace. Skirt is hand-embroidered, and doll
wears old ankle boots.

Projector with hand crank from the 1920s.

Maker unknown

Bisque, probably Kestner, 19-3/4 inches (50cm), marked
Gr.Nr.8. Made around 1890, doll is tinted bisque with
strongly tinted cheeks. Fixed, dark-brown glass eyes have
painted eyelashes and feathery, brown eyebrows. Mouth is
closed. Doll wears original human-hair wig. Shaped kid
leather body has molded porcelain hands. New costume
and bonnet are made of old fabric.

Maker unknown

Bisque, maker unknown, 21-3/4 inches (55cm). Made around 1885, turned-head doll has her slightly inclined head turned to the right. Doll is almost-white bisque, with apple-red cheeks. Fixed, blue glass eyes have painted eyelashes and painted eyebrows. Closed red-bow mouth has dimples. Doll wears old blond-mohair wig. New costume is made of old materials.

Maker unknown

Bisque, probably Kestner, 26-1/4 inches (67cm), marked
698 H 12. Made around 1885, shoulder-head doll has
molded bust, and cheeks are pink. Fixed, dark-brown glass
eyes have painted eyelashes and painted eyebrows. Mouth
is closed, and ears are pierced. Doll wears new
chestnut-colored human-hair wig. Body is leather with
bisque forearms. New costume is made of old materials.

Maker unknown

Bisque, probably Simon & Halbig, 15-3/4 inches (40cm).
Doll has molded bust of pale-pink tinted bisque. Sky-blue
glass eyes have rayed irises, painted eyelashes and painted
eyebrows. Mouth is closed, with red midline, and ears are
pierced. Doll wears original blond-mohair wig. Fabric
body has porcelain forearms. Costume is original.

Bisque Swivel-Head Dolls

Swivel-head dolls have movable heads, which made them fun to play with.

Teddy bear, named *Peter*, made in 1920, was not popular because children were frightened by his rolling eyes and grimace.

Heinrich Handwerck and Simon & Halbig

Bisque, Heinrich Handwerck and Simon & Halbig, 18-1/2 inches (47cm), marked *Heinrich Handwerck, Simon & Halbig*. Made around 1898, swivel-head doll is pink-tinted bisque with orange-tinted cheeks. Blue glass sleep eyes have rayed irises, painted eyelashes and molded, drawn eyebrows. Slightly open bow mouth has four teeth on top, and ears are pierced. Doll wears original gold-blond mohair wig. Composition body has 10 joints. Clothes are original.

This doll is shown in a different hat in close-up photo on opposite page and is described below.

Max Handwerck

Bisque, Max Handwerck, 25-1/2 inches (65cm), marked *Max Handwerck*. Made around 1910, swivel-head doll is rose-tinted bisque with pink cheeks. Gray-blue glass sleep eyes have rayed irises, painted eyelashes and painted eyebrows. Slightly open mouth has four teeth on top, with emphasized lines. Doll wears old blond-mohair wig. Composition body has 10 joints. New costume and hat are made of old hand-embroidered materials. Hat has old ostrich feather.

This doll is shown in close-up photo wearing hat on opposite page and is described below.

Alt, Beck & Gottschalk

Bisque, Alt, Beck & Gottschalk, 19-3/4 inches (50cm), marked *AB 1362 Made in Germany 1-1/2*. Made around 1919, swivel-head doll is pink-tinted bisque with rosy cheeks. Gray-blue glass sleep eyes have upper eyelashes of hair, painted lower eyelashes and painted brown eyebrows. Slightly open mouth has four teeth on top, and ears are pierced. Doll wears original mohair wig. Composition body has 10 joints. New costume is made of old materials.

Kämmer & Reinhardt

Bisque, Kämmer & Reinhardt, 15-1/4 inches (39cm),
marked *K&R 39*. Made around 1890, swivel-head doll is
pale-pink bisque with rosy cheeks. Sky-blue glass sleep
eyes have rayed irises, painted eyelashes and molded
brown eyebrows. Slightly open mouth has four teeth on
top, and ears are open. Doll wears old blond human-hair
wig. Composition body has 10 joints. New costume is
made of hand-embroidered materials.

Mail coach with wood draft horses, colorfully painted, made around 1900. Doll is shown in close-up photo on opposite page and is described below.

Kestner

Bisque, Kestner, Jr., 19-1/4 inches (49cm), Marked *JDK 214 made in Germany*. Made around 1910, swivel-head doll is tinted bisque with orange-red cheeks. Blue glass sleep eyes have rayed irises, painted eyelashes and strongly tinted eyebrows. Slightly open mouth has four teeth on top. Doll wears new human-hair wig. Composition body has 10 joints. New costume is made of old materials.

Kestner

Bisque, Kestner, 23-3/4 inches (60cm), marked *Germany B.5*. Made around 1900, swivel-head doll is pink-tinted bisque with brown-pink tinted cheeks. Brown glass sleep eyes have rayed irises, upper eyelashes of fur, painted lower eyelashes and painted eyebrows. Slightly open mouth has five teeth on top. Doll wears original hand-tied human-hair wig. Composition body has 10 joints. An old pattern was used to make reproduction costume of antique materials.

Doll from page 79 is shown with doll described below. Doll in blue is shown in full-length photo on opposite page.

Maker unknown

Bisque, maker unknown, 19-3/4 inches (50cm), marked 0. Made around 1905, swivel-head doll is pink-tinted bisque with strongly tinted cheeks. Gray glass sleep eyes have thread eyelashes, painted eyelashes and lightly tinted eyebrows. Open mouth has four teeth on top. Doll wears new mohair wig. Composition body has 10 joints. An old pattern was used to make reproduction costume of antique materials. English tin toys with markings are from the 1920s.

Lamb on wheels is made of real wool and has papier-mâché head with glass eyes. Possibly by Bing Brothers of Nuremberg, made around 1870. Height 14 inches (35cm). Doll is shown in close-up photo on opposite page and is described below.

Armand Marseille

Bisque, Armand Marseille, 25-1/2 inches (65cm), marked *1894 AM 10 DEP*. Made around 1894, swivel-head doll has tinted cheeks. Blue glass eyes have rayed irised with painted eyelashes and strongly tinted brown eyebrows. Open mouth has five teeth. Doll wears hand-tied original human-hair wig. Original composition jointed body has eight joints with extra-long thighs. Forearms and hands are one piece. Doll wears an old hat and clothes.

Biting dog with leather muzzle has body covered with real fur. Height is 11 inches (28cm). Doll on left is described below. Doll in middle is described on page 57. Doll on right is described on page 88.

Armand Marseille

Bisque, Armand Marseille, 19-3/4 inches (50cm), marked *1894 DEP*. Made around 1895, swivel-head doll is tinted-pink bisque with tinted cheeks and chin dimple. Gray eyes have rayed irises with black border, painted eyelashes and painted brown eyebrows. Pink open mouth has three teeth, and one tooth is missing. Doll wears original hand-tied human-hair wig. Narrow composition body has extra-long straight thighs. Costume is old fabric with crocheted lace and waistband of old beading.

Doll photographed with windmill and flowers is shown in close-up photo on opposite page and is described below.

Armand Marseille

Bisque, Armand Marseille, 17-3/4 inches (45cm), marked *AM 1894 3 DEP made in Germany*. This swivel-head doll is light bisque. She has fixed black eyes. Slightly open mouth has four teeth on top. Doll wears original hand-tied human-hair wig. French stiff-jointed composition body has eight joints. Costume is original, and arms of blouse were restored with antique lace.

Doll with magic-lantern disk made around 1880 by Ernst Planck of Nuremberg.
Doll is shown with lamb in photo on opposite page and is described below.

Armand Marseille

Bisque, Armand Marseille, 17 inches (43cm), marked *390 A.2 M made in Germany*. Made around 1900, swivel-head doll has pink cheeks and chin dimples. Fawn-colored glass eyes have painted eyelashes and molded, shaded eyebrows. Slightly open bow-shaped mouth has four teeth on top. Doll wears original auburn human-hair wig. Composition body has 10 joints. New costume is made of old materials.

Doll photographed with spinning wheel is shown in close-up photo on opposite page and is described below.

Armand Marseille

Bisque, Armand Marseille, 12-1/2 inches (32cm), marked *Armand Marseille Germany 390*. Made around 1902, swivel-head doll has pink cheeks. Blue glass sleep eyes have hair eyelashes on top lids, painted lower eyelashes and painted eyebrows. Open mouth has four teeth on top. Doll wears old mohair wig. New costume is made of old materials.

French Jumeau doll in old hammock, 15-3/4 inches (40cm) long. Doll is shown in photo on opposite page with doll described below.

Armand Marseille

Bisque, Armand Marseille, 13-3/4 inches (35cm), marked *1894 AM DEP made in Germany*. Made around 1895, swivel-head doll has strongly tinted cheeks and chin dimples. Dark-brown glass sleep eyes have painted eyelashes and painted eyebrows. Slightly open mouth has four teeth on top. Doll wears original mohair wig. Composition body has eight joints, and arms and hands are one piece. New costume is made of old materials. Doll is seated on painted Hungarian horse. Large doll is French Jumeau.

Two doll umbrellas. Black-silk umbrella has brass knobs and is 7-3/4 inches (20cm) long. Printed-cotton umbrella is 9-3/4 inches (25cm) long. Umbrellas were made around 1900.

Anger and Moehling

Bisque, Anger and Moehling, 31-1/2 inches (80cm), marked *15 A&M Made in Austria*. We include this Austrian doll by Anger and Moehling (A&M) because it is often falsely attributed to the German doll maker, Armand Marseille. Made around 1904, swivel-head doll is delicately tinted bisque with pink cheeks. Fixed, cobalt-blue glass eyes have rayed irises. Slightly open bow mouth has four teeth on top. Doll wears original human-hair wig. Composition body has 10 joints. Costume is child's old clothes.

Three dolls in a toy boat. Doll on left is shown in close-up photo on opposite page and is described below. Doll in middle is AM 390, page 91. Doll on right is French Jumeau.

Ohlhaver Brothers

Bisque, Ohlhaver Brothers, 21-3/4 inches (55cm), marked *Revalo 8-1/2 made in Germany*. Made around 1915, swivel-head doll is pink-tinted bisque with strongly tinted cheeks. Blue eyes have black lashes, painted lower lashes and lightly waved eyebrows. Slightly open mouth has four teeth on top. Doll wears original human-hair wig. Composition body has 10 joints. Costume is old.

Doll shown with two 19th-century Indian horses that are hand-carved and hand-finished. She is shown without hat in close-up photo on opposite page and is described below.

Schoenau & Hoffmeister

Bisque, Schoenau & Hoffmeister, 27-1/2 inches (70cm), marked *S(starPB)H*. Made around 1906, swivel-head doll has pink cheeks. Gray-blue glass sleep eyes have rayed irises, upper eyelashes of hair, as well as painted upper and lower eyelashes, and painted light-brown eyebrows. Slightly open bow mouth has four teeth on top. Doll wears original chestnut-brown mohair wig. Composition body has 10 joints. New costume is made of old materials.

Doll standing in field of flowers is shown in another costume in close-up photo on opposite page and is described below.

Simon & Halbig

Bisque, Simon & Halbig, 23-3/4 inches (60cm), marked *SH1079/12 DEP*. Made around 1892, swivel-head doll is delicately tinted bisque. Blue glass sleep eyes have dark-blue rims and rayed irises, painted eyelashes and painted brown eyebrows. Open bow mouth has four teeth on top, and molded ears are pierced. Doll wears new human-hair wig. Composition body has 10 joints. New costume is made of old materials.

Doll with butterfly wings is shown in close-up photo on opposite page and is described below.

Simon & Halbig

Bisque, Simon & Halbig, 12-1/4 inches (31cm), marked *S&H 3-1/2*. Made around 1905, swivel-head doll has strongly tinted cheeks. Blue glass sleep eyes have painted eyelashes and painted eyebrows. Open mouth has four teeth, and ears are pierced. Doll wears original human-hair wig. Composition body has 10 joints. New costume is made of new materials.

Chicken is made of colored felt and stands 7 inches (18cm) tall. Doll on left is shown in another costume in close-up photo on opposite page and is described below. Doll on right is shown in another wig on page 75.

Simon & Halbig

Bisque, Simon & Halbig, 18 inches (46cm), marked *1078 Simon & Halbig 6-1/2 Germany*. Made around 1900, swivel-head doll has rosy cheeks. Brown glass sleep eyes have rayed irises, painted eyelashes on lower lids, hair eyelashes on upper lids and molded brown eyebrows. Open mouth has four teeth, and ears are pierced. Doll wears original blond human-hair wig. Composition body has 10 joints. Black-and-red costume was made after 1900.

Bisque Character Dolls

In the first decade of the 20th century, realistic character dolls were introduced. Maybe people were bored with cute little dolls. Dolls that were beautiful-ugly, such as the *Kaiser baby*, page 133, were made and sold with great success. They were followed by character dolls that were beautiful, and these are popular today with collectors. Character dolls look so lifelike, you might mistake one for a living child at first glance.

Wicker doll sofa, 13-3/4 inches (35cm) long, made around 1915. Doll on sofa is shown on opposite page with smaller doll and is described below.

Kämmer & Reinhardt and Simon & Halbig

Bisque, Kämmer & Reinhardt, Simon & Halbig, 21-1/4 inches (54cm), marked *Nr. 117 A, 54.* Swivel-head doll has pink-tinted bisque with rosy cheeks. Gray-blue glass sleep eyes have rayed irises, painted eyelashes and painted eyebrows. Mouth is closed. Doll wears original blond-mohair wig. Composition body has 10 joints. Costume is original. Small doll is 11 inches (28cm).

Kämmer & Reinhardt
and Simon & Halbig

Bisque, Kämmer & Reinhardt, Simon & Halbig, 31-1/2 inches (80cm), marked *K (star)R Simon & Halbig 117 N Germany 80.* Made around 1920, swivel-head doll has brown-red cheeks and chin dimple. Gray-blue glass flirty sleep eyes have painted eyelashes and feathered brown eyebrows. Open mouth has teeth. Doll wears original blond-mohair wig. Composition body has 10 joints and rubber hands. Clothes are child's old clothes.

No.1448 of Simon & Halbig is the star of this book. She is one of the most-beautiful, rarest and most-desirable German dolls. Her face is realistic, charming and graceful. She might be mistaken for a living child.

Simon & Halbig

Bisque, Simon & Halbig, 19-3/4 inches (50cm), marked *1448 Simon & Halbig, S&H*. Made around 1905, swivel-head doll has rosy cheeks. Brown glass sleep eyes have rayed irises, painted eyelashes and painted brown eyebrows. Closed mouth has accentuated midline, and ears are pierced. Doll wears original mohair wig. Composition body has 10 joints. Old costume includes lace stockings and leather boots.

Maker unknown

Bisque, probably Bruno Schmidt, 15-3/4 inches (40cm), marked *182*. Character doll with swivel head is pink-tinted bisque with rosy cheeks. Painted blue eyes have painted eyelashes, painted eyebrows and brown lid lines. Mouth is closed. Doll wears light-blond mohair wig. Composition body has 10 joints. New costume is made of old materials.

Heubach Brothers

Bisque, Heubach Brothers, 12-1/2 inches (32cm), marked 6/0. Made around 1910, swivel-head doll has rosy cheeks. Painted brown eyes have brown lid lines and brown eyebrows. Mouth is closed in a pout. Blond hair is molded. Composition toddler's body has 10 joints. Costume was made after 1910.

Armand Marseille

Below: Bisque, Armand Marseille, 12-1/2 inches (32cm), marked *Germany 323 M2/0M*. Made around 1915, swivel-head Googly doll has pink cheeks. Brown glass sleep eyes have painted eyelashes and painted eyebrows. Mouth is closed. Doll wears original hand-tied human-hair wig. Composition baby's body has four joints. Costume is old cotton clothing.

Armand Marseille

Doll on left on opposite page: Bisque, Armand Marseille, 9 inches (23cm), marked *323 A. 6/0 made in Germany*. Made around 1918, swivel-head Googly doll has pink cheeks and chin dimple. Blue glass sleep eyes have rayed irises, roguish eyes, painted eyelashes and painted brown eyebrows. Closed mouth has sly smile. Doll wears original blond-mohair wig. Composition body has a little tummy and six joints. Costume and underwear are old.

Maker unknown

Doll on right on opposite page: Bisque, maker unknown, 7 inches (18cm). Made around 1915, swivel-head Googly doll has pink cheeks. Brown roguish sleep eyes have painted eyelashes and painted eyebrows. Closed mouth has impish smile. Doll wears original mohair wig. Body is all bisque with four joints, molded stockings and shoes. Costume includes old silk shawl. Googlies were made by several doll makers. Large eyes were called *roguish*. Children loved these dolls.

Oriental and Exotic Bisque Dolls

Dolls with different skin colors or those dressed to represent peoples of other lands were popular with young and old doll lovers. Dolls were made to represent Burmese, Japanese, Indians and Negroes.

Kämmer & Reinhardt and Simon & Halbig

Bisque, Kämmer & Reinhardt, Simon & Halbig, marked *K(star)R Simon & Halbig 126*. Made around 1915, swivel-head black baby doll is dark-brown bisque. Dark-brown glass sleep eyes have painted eyelashes and painted eyebrows. Open mouth has two teeth on top. Doll wears original black-mohair wig. Brown composition baby body has four joints.

Kestner

Bisque, Kestner, Jr., 16-1/2 inches (42cm), marked 98/4 *made in Germany*. Made around 1910, swivel-head black doll is black-tinted bisque. Gold-brown glass sleep eyes have rayed irises, painted eyelashes and painted black eyebrows. Open mouth has two teeth on top, and ears are pierced. Doll wears original hand-tied human-hair wig. Brown composition body has 10 joints.

Oriental dolls. Small doll on left is described on page 124. Doll on right is shown in close-up photo on opposite page and is described below.

Kestner

Bisque, Kestner, Jr., 19-3/4 inches (50cm), marked *164, Germany, 38 Orientalin*. Made around 1900, swivel-head doll is yellow-tinted bisque, with lightly tinted pink cheeks. Brown glass sleep eyes have painted eyelashes and plumed brows. Open mouth has four teeth. Doll wears original black-mohair wig. Shaped leather body has porcelain forearms. Silk costume is original.

Lathe-turned wood chair with painted gold-bronze trim and flowers, upholstered with silk.

Simon & Halbig

Bisque, Simon & Halbig, 11-3/4 inches (30cm), marked *Simon & Halbig 1329, 2, Orientalin, Made in Germany.* Made around 1900, swivel-head doll is yellow-tinted bisque with pink cheeks. Brown glass sleep eyes have painted eyelashes and molded eyebrows. Slightly open mouth has four teeth, and ears are pierced. Doll wears original black-mohair wig. Yellow-tinted jointed composition body has 10 joints. Silk costume is original.

Armand Marseille

Bisque, Armand Marseille, 11-3/4 inches (30cm), marked *A.M. Germany 341/3*. Made around 1923, black baby doll has flange-neck head. Dark bisque has black-hair base. Dark brown glass sleep eyes have painted eyelashes and painted eyebrows. Closed mouth is red. Brown fabric baby body has "Mama" voice and papier-mâché hands. Costume is old.

Bisque Baby Dolls

Baby dolls were first made in 1875 for children to use when playing house—little girls could be doll mothers. The beauty of baby dolls ranged from beautiful-ugly to adorable. The success of character baby dolls was heightened when dolls were given movable sleep eyes in 1914.

Heubach of Köppelsdorf

Bisque, Heubach of Köppelsdorf, 18-1/2 inches (47cm), marked *Heubach Köppelsdorf Nr. 342.3 Germany II*. Tinted bisque with orange-red cheeks. Gray-blue glass sleep eyes have painted eyelashes and painted eyebrows. Open mouth has two large teeth on top. Doll wears original hand-tied blond-mohair wig. Composition baby body has four joints. New costume is made of new materials.

Kämmer & Reinhardt and Simon & Halbig

Bisque, Kämmer & Reinhardt, Simon & Halbig, 12-1/4 inches (31cm), marked *K&R Simon & Halbig 122*. Made around 1920, swivel-head doll has pink cheeks. Brown glass sleep eyes have painted eyelashes and painted eyebrows. Slightly open mouth has two teeth on top. Doll wears original hand-tied human-hair wig. Baby body has four joints. New crochet clothing is made of old materials.

Kämmer & Reinhardt

Doll on left on opposite page: Bisque, Kämmer & Reinhardt, 14-1/4 inches (36cm), marked *36 K&R 100*. Made around 1909, this swivel-head character baby doll was later called *Kaiser baby*. Doll is tinted bisque and mouth is open-closed. Eyes are painted blue, and hair is painted at base. Composition baby body has four joints. Costume is old.

Otto Reinecke

Doll on right on opposite page and above: Bisque, Otto Reinecke, 14-1/4 inches, (36cm), marked *P.M. 914,5*. Made around 1905, swivel-head character doll has pink cheeks. Pale-gray glass sleep eyes have painted eyelashes and rising eyebrows. Open mouth has one tooth missing on top and molded tongue. Doll wears new human-hair wig. Composition standing baby body has four joints. Costume is old.

Doll carriage with gray-blue lacquer hood and iron wheels, made around 1890.
Doll in carriage is shown on opposite page and is described below. Standing
next to the carriage is French Jumeau doll.

Armand Marseille

Bisque, Armand Marseille, 17-3/4 inches (45cm), marked
AM 341. Made around 1923, and called *My Dream Baby*,
swivel-head doll is tinted bisque. Blue sleep eyes have
painted eyelashes and painted eyebrows. Mouth is closed.
Molded hair is painted. Baby body is composition. New
baby clothes are made of new material.

Dog with glass eyes and cheerful costume. Height 13-3/4 inches (35cm), made around 1920.

Kämmer & Reinhardt

Bisque, Kämmer & Reinhardt, 16-1/2 inches (42cm), marked K(star)R 126 Germany 42. Made around 1920, swivel-head character baby doll has apple-red cheeks and chin dimple. Gold-brown glass sleep eyes have rayed irises, painted eyelashes and painted eyebrows. Open mouth has two teeth on top. Doll wears new human-hair wig. Composition baby body has four joints. New costume is made of old materials.

Laughing or crying is not a problem for this multiface doll. Child can play with doll no matter what mood she is in! Sleep-face doll originated with Bergner's three-faced doll. Wood cylinder turns head.

Bergner

Bisque, Bergner, 11 inches (28cm), marked *C.B.* Three faces of doll show it laughing, crying and sleeping. Swivel-head doll has painted eyelashes, molded teardrops and fixed, brown eyes. Mouth is closed. Outer shell of hair is papier-mâché with mohair locks. Fabric body has composition limbs. Dress and bonnet are original.

Mechanical, Semiautomatic and Automatic Dolls

Doll makers took into account a child's desire to play when they decided to make mechanical dolls that did interesting things. Some dolls danced, drank or talked. Some made music, and there were other variations. Doll makers usually depended on distributors for supplies of technical and mechanical equipment. They did not make these devices themselves.

Partially painted balancing figure made around 1890.

Heubach Brothers

Bisque, Heubach Brothers, 13 inches (21cm). Made around 1900, semiautomatic doll has crank that makes doll clap hands together and bells ring, while melody plays. Bisque head has molded blond-painted hair. Eyes are painted brown. Open-closed mouth has two molded bottom teeth. Costume is original.

Bisque Dollhouse Dolls

Because dollhouses were small, little bisque dolls that could be played with in dollhouses were popular. Painting on these dolls was not as precise as painting on larger bisque dolls. Dollhouse dolls were an important element in the different types of dolls made.

Parlor arrangement of four unmarked bisque dolls, with molded, painted hair, and shoes and stockings.

Maker unknown

Bisque, maker unknown, 5 inches (12cm). Made around 1880, the *Grödner doll* is from the Grödner valley in the south Tyrol. Doll has wood body and bisque head. Eyes, eyebrows, mouth and cheeks are painted. Crudely carved wood body has four limbs, and head is held on by wires. Legs are painted. Painted iron rocking chair is 6 inches (15cm) high.

Simon & Halbig

Bisque, Simon & Halbig, 11-1/2 inches (29cm), marked
S&H 1160/0. Made around 1870, shoulder-head doll has
pink cheeks. Fixed brown glass eyes have painted
eyelashes and painted eyebrows. Mouth is closed. Doll
wears original mohair wig with corkscrew curls. Leather
body has bisque forearms. New costume is made of old
materials.

Dollhouses

The existence of dollhouses goes back to ancient Greece and Rome. In Germany, there is proof of a dollhouse from 1558 that Albrecht V of Bavaria had made for his daughter. Dollhouses of the 19th century were often architectural works of art. This was true for dollhouses made by German, Dutch, French, English and Italian makers. Rooms were furnished with beautifully made miniature furniture. An elegantly furnished salon, with silk rugs, fireplace and furniture, was as common as furnished bedrooms, kitchen and dining room.

Half-Dolls and Knickknack Dolls

Freed of tea cozies and pincushions, delicate half-dolls are popular collectables. Half-dolls and knickknack dolls can be found in china or bisque.

Maker unknown

Bisque, maker unknown, 5 inches (13cm). Made around 1920, unmarked nude model doll is delicately tinted bisque. Hair and bow are molded bisque and painted. Red plush sofa is 6-1/4x10-1/2 inches (16x27cm).

Doll furniture shown with bisque doll.

Bisque half-dolls and knickknack dolls from the 1920s.

China-head half-dolls. Heights range from 1-1/2 inches to 4-3/4 inches (4 to 12cm).

Doll Scenes in Color Prints

Dolls were often used when a child was the subject of prints, watercolors, oil paintings or other art pieces. Art pieces are documents of the times and contain details significant to cultural history. They are rewarding to collect.

Doll's mother, from a painting by D. Piltz

Small vanity, from a painting by F. C. Hoesch

Dolls in Photography

Whether 1870 or 1920, when a child had his or her picture taken, a doll was often used as a calming influence. Exhibited on post cards, which became popular after the turn of the century, a doll often played a central role.

Child photographed with favorite doll

Photo post cards often told stories. Post cards have not yet been discovered by doll collectors as collectable items.

Doll Scenes on Post Cards and Collectors' Cards

Sentimental post cards with doll scenes were published as art post cards by companies such as Pauli Ebner. Collectors' pictures, which were published by many firms and carried doll scenes, were common.

Post cards from 1908

Poems and Stories

Many poems and stories deal with doll themes and should be preserved. Here are a few samples from *Kinderwelt (Child's World)* magazine of 1926 to 1927.

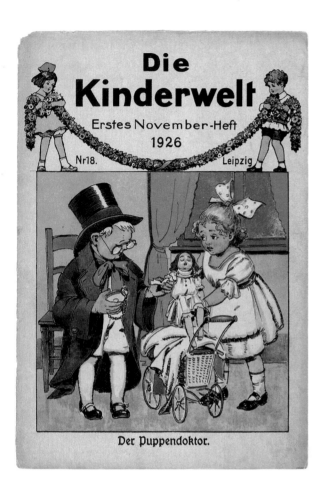

Die Kinderwelt
Erstes November-Heft
1926
Nr 18.   Leipzig

Der Puppendoktor.

The Doll Doctor

"How good, dear doctor, that you have come,
I have waited for you a long time.
My darling child is giving me quite a worry,
And her state of health is making me uneasy.
Early today all was quite pleasant,
Quite fresh and lively while we played.
Then she knocked herself on her delicate little nose,
And a little piece fell off."
"Now, now, Mrs. Neighbor, let me show you
What will be a good idea to do.
Yes, yes, she seems ill, still to be sure,
I will heal her after a short period of time.
But here? Does that not seem best to you?
This is certainly a very bad thing.
The small rip in the little leather leg,
Do not bump it even a little.
The wound is still quite serious
For one who is as small as she.
In any case I must sew it up.
Otherwise it would soon be much worse.
I have put on a good cast
And tomorrow I will bring a sewing machine.
The little doll must lie still
And may not move a single step."
"Oh no, dear Doctor, I am upset
About this littlest, most-delicate child.
I beg you, do your best
And I hope she will heal quickly."

Hedwig Muller

Two Quarreling Sisters

Two quarreling little hens,
Little Susanne and Little Louise,
Two sisters, as you know,
Received a doll for Christmas.
They should have played with her
In a nice, sisterly way,
But the naughty little girls
Thought only of arguing with each other.
Soon one hit the other,
And the other hit back.
Soon one wanted to pull the doll away,
And the other pulled it back.
Then Mama said angrily,
"You are giving me no thanks."
She took the doll
And stuck her in the cupboard.

Unsociable

A new little doll, so elegant and fine
Was brought into the room by little Lottie.
The old doll murmured, "Oh, no,
I would rather be left all alone!"
Then Lottie heard the new doll say,
"Come, let us be sociable
And really love one another,
So that our little mother will not be troubled."
The old doll spoke angrily,
"Go away! I do not like you!"
The little mother argued, "Shame on you,
So naughty and already so big.
Now you must stay in the corner!
I don't want to see such a bad child!"

Uncle Hans

Learn Order!

From *The Child's World*, 1927, by Von Helene and Walter Jensen

All three were in bed, the little boy and two little girls. They were washed and asleep in their white beds. It seemed so peaceful, as if the little ones could not stir. But you should have seen what they did!

The toys from Christmas—how they had been mistreated! The building blocks were in a box, and the box had been rolled under the bed. In the doll carriage were a jump rope, tennis racket, two balls and a piano, whose top had been ripped off because the boy had wanted to see what was inside. Dolls were in the wash basin, and one wig still hung on the window frame.

The moon looked in the window and smiled with his agreeable face on the three sleeping children. As he became aware of the disorder in the room, his face creased with a frown. He saw the teddy bear on the floor, on its muzzle so it sneezed three times. Teddy began to growl, then dance. He bumped the scalped doll, Liselotte, with his muzzle and said, "Look how the children lie in their beds so comfortably. But they have thrown us into every corner, some here, some there, hurt and tattered, as if they had no sense of order. They do not know where they last left us. Is that not a burden?"

Crying, Liselotte answered, "Mama." That was all she knew how to say. She only said, "Mama."

"Also an answer," growled Teddy and trotted away.

The elephant trumpeted, "Pay attention! You have stepped on my second most-sensitive corn!"

"Excuse me," said Teddy. "Why are you lying in the middle of the floor?"

The elephant said, "Because the little boy is so sloppy! He threw me here. Look—my left hind leg is out of joint!"

As Teddy looked at it, tin soldiers called from one of the corners, "Ouch! Our broken legs hurt so much!" And the beads, for beautiful handwork, rattled in boxes that were lying around. The doll carriage rolled around the room by itself.

The rocking horse whinnied and galloped while the piano played, "Hop, hop, hop, little horse

run and gallop!" While all this was going on, balls flew around the room. It *was* a spectacle!

But the children were sleeping so deeply they did not notice anything. Jutta turned on her side. Susie kicked her covers away. Norbert stuck his thumb in his mouth.

Then the moon said to the toys, "You can make as much noise as you want! It will not waken them! The sandman has put them deeply asleep so they can become big and strong. But you should punish them for their sloppiness and slovenliness. Pull them out of their beds so they sleep on the floor. Then you can lie in the soft beds! That will help. Perhaps they will become orderly children!"

The clever moon's advice cheered the toys. They climbed on Jutta's bed. The moon shone so they could see. The rocking horse grasped Jutta's big toe with his teeth. Teddy took her arm with his paw. Another doll and Liselotte grabbed a tuft of hair. The tin soldiers pushed her hard from behind. The puppet shouted, "One, two, three!" and Jutta fell with a thud to the rug.

The same thing happened to Susie and Norbert, and the moon shone on them all. Then the toys arranged themselves in the bed and went to sleep. The children were not aware of the change, and the smiling moon plodded on his way.

As Mother Sun spread out her beautiful rays the next morning, the children awoke. Susie blinked first and said, "My mattress is very hard!"

Norbert sat up and asked, "Where is my pillow?"

Jutta sat up and leaned on the bedpost. She called, "Nana!"

All three cried as if with a single voice, "Mommy!" They believed their mother had put them out of bed as a punishment. How astonished they were when they discovered their mother knew nothing about it.

As soon as the puppet, who had had the best place on Susie's pillow, cried, "Ha Ha" loudly and distinctly, the children realized the toys would never be subjected to such bad treatment again.

From then on, the three children put their toys away before going to sleep. And they never again awoke on the floor.

Leipzig Doll Doctor

Excerpt from article by Emil Schmidt in 1874 in *Illustrierte Welt (Illustrated World)*.

The rooms of the apartment were filled with doll inhabitants. Wherever one looked, everything was full—wild!—with dolls. The little friendly lady is the Leipzig Doll Doctor herself. Yes, the Doll Doctor! The title does not go far enough in describing her profession thoroughly: Our poodle on the table, whom she helped again to his feet, bears witness that she is a true helper of our beloved toys.

The Doll Doctor lives, as I made my visit with sketch book under my arm, in the old school lane. On one door was the name Schneider. After repeated knocks, a voice said the usual, "Come in!" A moment in the apartment told me I was in the right place. Seeing my anxious expression, the Doll Doctor imparted a friendly manner. I had chosen the most fortunate time: three or four weeks before Christmas, in the year 1873. The business was in full flower. There were so many patients, I had to get my eyes used to the situation before I could find my way around.

All day long we worked together, she on her chair, executing the most difficult operations and wonderful cures with the greatest ease and surety. I squatted on a footstool and drew row upon row of dolls in my sketchbook. Indeed, I had seen everything. Truly, the cures of the world-renowned, arrogant braggart, Dr. Eisenbart, were nothing in comparison. With at least equal love, equal regard and touching devotion, the doll patients, one after another, without respect to person or origin, were cured without any preceding clamor or fanfare. And the doctor's bill? Truly, no one had anything to complain about.

There were patients with lost heads, and the heads were put back on them again. Or the old doll body was decorated with a new little head. Shattered or broken limbs were repaired or sometimes new ones were put on.

Whenever a doll had lost her hair, she was sent to the hairdresser because our wonderful doctor needed an assistant in matters of heads of hair. Over there was a maiden with a shabby body who, according to how she was turned, modestly opened and closed her eyes and looked forward impatiently to the thing that should happen there. Whoever had faded red cheeks, whoever had acquired wrinkles due to life's struggles, whoever had worn out or broken her nose—our Doll Doctor magically fixed them.

She added a new complexion, roses and cream cheeks, lips like rosy embers, the nose in a noble form—in short the whole freshness of youth, not to forget the positioning of little earrings through her ex-

cellent handling. Whoever had eyes that could no longer look up, and oh, my goodness, those were many, or whoever had a pair of holes in the head instead of eyes, she carefully pulled the skull apart, polished the windows of the soul, put them back or replaced them with a new pair, and checked to make sure the seeing apparatus performed its customary laughing duty. Whoever had a voice that failed for lack of breath, a new breath was blown in, and once again the little crying doll squeaked and squealed her "papa" and "mama." I will desist from enumerating all the wonder cures. I bid you: go and see for yourself!

While we worked, our conversation went this way and that, though still it could not come in a true flow with the best determination, because—I am not lying—a whole five minutes had ensued from the knock at the door, the natural response "Come In!" and then a visit.

The people who came there! Big and little, old and young, poor and rich, in short the whole human race sent its representatives, and only in the rarest of instances did the good doctor lady send someone away without hope. Day and night the wonder-cures never ceased because the good-natured woman represented a considerable skill. She did not take a break until two

or three in the morning. This continued, beginning many weeks before Christmas, day after day until the holiday, when she would be able to rest on her deserved laurels and take a vacation.

The penetrating glance and overview with which she surveyed her doll hospital was worthy of wonder. Many of the dolls were unnumbered, but many had distinctive markings. However, no mistake came of it, no mixing up. No matter how distinguished and exalted their cures were, the not-uniquely existing circumstance throughout taught that the cured dolls were hardly or not at all recognized again by the recipient. Still, the conscientiousness and expert eye of our doll doctor can be relied upon because she is like a mother with her child in the way she knows her charges. She always knows who they are, where they came from and to whom they belong.

Even if the summer house had room left over for it, who could exhibit all of those who through their visits experienced further renewing, stimulating and enlivening scenes in the doll hospital? And so we depart from the subject of our illustration with the wish that the Doll Doctor lady might still see her healing institution populated for a long time to come for the joy of our children's world.

Index

7.3892407429